FROM HOPE TO JOY

FROM
HOPE
TO
JOY

Services of Worship and Additional Resources
for the Seasons of Advent and Christmas
with Introduction and Commentary

SUPPLEMENTAL WORSHIP RESOURCES 15

Don E. Saliers

ABINGDON PRESS
Nashville
1984

FROM HOPE TO JOY

Library of Congress Cataloging in Publication Data

SALIERS, DON E., 1937–
    From hope to joy.
    (Supplemental worship resources 15)
    1. United Methodist Church (U.S.)—Liturgy—Texts.
    2. Methodist Church—Liturgy—Texts. I. Title.
    II. Series.
BX8337.S24   1984   264'.076   83-21383

ISBN 0-687-13644-X

Scripture quotations unless otherwise noted are from the Revised Standard Version of the Bible,
copyrighted 1946, 1952, © 1971, 1973 by the Division of Christian Education of the National
Council of the Churches of Christ in the U.S.A. and used by permission.

The text from the hymn by Charles Wesley on pages 35-36 is from Ernest J. Rattenbury, *The
Eucharistic Hymns of John and Charles Wesley.*

The Collect for the Second Sunday in Advent on page 69 is reprinted from the Lutheran *Service
Book and Hymnal*, Copyright 1958, by permission of Augsburg Publishing House.

The verses on page 75 are from "Light One Candle," from *Sunday Songbook* by Natalie Sleeth;
copyright © 1976 by Hinshaw Music, Inc., Chapel Hill, NC 27514. Used by permission 12/15/83.

The translation of Psalm 72:1-14 on pages 99-100 is from Gary Chamberlain, *The Psalter*
(forthcoming 1984), used by permission of the publisher, The Upper Room, P.O. Box 189,
Nashville, TN 37202.

The following sections are adapted from The Book of Common Prayer of The Episcopal Church:
the Collect for All Saints' Day (p. 13), Psalm 24:1-6 (pp. 13-14), the Postcommunion Prayer (p. 39),
the third Collect for Christmas Day (p. 82), Eucharistic Prayer D (pp. 127-30), the Collects for
Advent and for the Christmas and Epiphany Seasons (pp. 133-37), and the Litany of Thanksgiving
(p. 137).

Material from *Seasons of the Gospel*, Copyright © 1979 by Abingdon, and *At the Lord's Table*,
Copyright © 1972, 1976, 1979, 1980 by The United Methodist Publishing House, is scattered
throughout. Used by permission.

The lines on pages 54-55 are from "At Last Night Is Ending," from *Prayers, Poems, and Songs* by
Huub Oosterhuis, copyright by Herder and Herder 1970. By permission of Uitgeverij Ambo bv,
Baarn, Holland.

MANUFACTURED BY THE PARTHENON PRESS AT
NASHVILLE, TENNESSEE, UNITED STATES OF AMERICA

CONTENTS

PREFACE

From Hope to Joy is the fifteenth in the Supplemental Worship Resources series (SWR)—originally called the Alternate Rituals series—developed and sponsored by the Section on Worship of the Board of Discipleship of The United Methodist Church.

When The United Methodist Church was formed in 1968, *The Book of Discipline* (Par. 1388) stated that

> the hymnals of The United Methodist Church are the hymnals of The Evangelical United Brethren Church and *The Methodist Hymnal* [later retitled *The Book of Hymns*]; the Ritual of the Church is that contained in the *Book of Ritual* of The Evangelical United Brethren Church, 1959, and *The Book of Worship for Church and Home* of The Methodist Church.

It quickly became apparent, however, that there was a need for supplemental worship resources which, while not taking the place of these official resources, would provide alternatives to more fully reflect developments in the contemporary ecumenical church. The General Conference of 1970 authorized the Commission on Worship to begin work in this area, and the General Conferences of 1972 and 1976 authorized the Board of Discipleship "to

7

develop standards and resources for the conduct of public worship in the churches" (1976 *Book of Discipline*, Par. 1316.2).

The resulting series of publications began with *The Sacrament of The Lord's Supper: An Alternate Text*, 1972 (SWR 1), which was published both in a Text Edition and later (1975) in a Music Edition. Intensive work during the next four years led to the publication in 1976 of *A Service of Baptism, Confirmation, and Renewal: An Alternate Text*, 1976 (SWR 2), *Word and Table: A Basic Pattern of Sunday Worship for United Methodists* (SWR 3), and *Ritual in a New Day: An Invitation* (SWR 4). In 1973 the process of development was begun for *A Service of Christian Marriage* (SWR 5) and *A Service of Death and Resurrection* (SWR 7), both published in 1979.

In 1977 plans were made to publish three books dealing with the Christian Year. *Seasons of the Gospel*, Resources for the Christian Year (SWR 6), and *From Ashes to Fire*, Services of Worship for the Seasons of Lent and Easter, with Introduction and Commentary (SWR 8), were published in 1979. *From Hope to Joy* (SWR 15), although delayed in its publication, completes this treatment of the Christian Year.

Meanwhile, the series has continued with *At the Lord's Table*, a Communion Service Book for Use by the Minister (SWR 9); *We Gather Together: Services of Public Worship*, a booklet for pew use (SWR 10); *Supplement to The Book of Hymns* (SWR 11); *Songs of Zion*, a songbook from the black religious tradition (SWR 12); *Hymns from the Four Winds*, a Collection of Asian American Hymns (SWR 13); and *Blessings and Consecrations: A Book of Occasional Services* (SWR 14).

From Hope to Joy builds upon the theological and pastoral understanding of Sunday worship presented in *Word and Table* and the resources for the Christian Year presented in *Seasons of the Gospel*. The reader can profitably read both these volumes as a basis for understanding and using the present volume.

Like the other publications in this series, *From Hope to Joy* represents the corporate work of the writers and consultants, with the Section on Worship acting as an editorial committee. This committee determined the original specifications and carefully examined and edited the manuscript before approving it for publication.

Don E. Saliers, Ph.D., of Emory University was the principal writer of the manuscript. Kenneth Bedell, M. Div., pastor of The Preston United Methodist Parish, Preston, Maryland, researched the background and wrote the chapter on John Wesley's covenant service. During the writing, consultations were held with Hoyt L. Hickman, D.D., of the Board of Discipleship staff, James F. White, Ph.D., and Susan White, M.A. The manuscript was read by members of the Section on Worship, who made helpful suggestions. We wish to mention especially Janet A. Lee and D. S. Dharmapalan, B.D. Valuable assistance was given by Carlton R. Young, Ph.D., and Timothy Albrecht, D.F.A., concerning the service music, hymn texts, and psalmody. And Janet Gary, with expertise and unfailing good cheer, helped to prepare the manuscript.

The members and staff of the Section on Worship, listed below, wish to thank the persons named above and many others who have shared ideas and resources for the seasons of Advent and Christmas. Reactions to this volume—comments or suggestions—and any materials that have been created or discovered are welcomed by the Section on Worship, P.O. Box 840, Nashville, TN 37202. We commend this volume to the use of local churches in the hope that it will be helpful in the worship of God and the proclamation of the gospel of Jesus Christ.

Members of the Section on Worship: Stan DePano (chairperson), George W. Watson (vice-chairperson), D. S. Dharmapalan (secretary), Bishop George W. Bashore,

Donald Bueg, Carole Cotton-Winn, Melissa Lynn Ives, J. Sue Kana-Mackey, Merwin Kurtz, Mary Penn, Luis Sotomayor, Sharon Spieth, and Langill Watson.

Representing the Fellowship of United Methodists in Worship, Music, and Other Arts: Janet A. Lee (president) and Patty Evans (executive secretary-treasurer).

Staff of the Section on Worship: Ezra Earl Jones (general secretary), Noe E. Gonzales (associate general secretary), Hoyt L. Hickman (assistant general secretary), Richard L. Eslinger, Barbara P. Garcia, and Judy L. Loehr.

List of Hymnbook Abbreviations

BOH	*The Book of Hymns*
EP	*Ecumenical Praise*
HFW	*Hymns from the Four Winds*
LBW	*Lutheran Book of Worship*
SBH	*Supplement to The Book of Hymns*
SZ	*Songs of Zion*

PRE-ADVENT SERVICES IN NOVEMBER:
Orders of Worship with Commentaries

Three days in November, prior to the first Sunday of Advent, deserve special attention. Two are festival days that developed historically in the Christian West. The third—Thanksgiving—is a national holiday celebrated by citizens of the United States. All three days have deep religious and theological significance, and so deserve special care in planning.

All Saints' Day falls on November 1, but may be celebrated on the first Sunday in November. The last Sunday of the Season After Pentecost is called the Feast of Christ the King and may occur between November 20 and 26, inclusive. Thanksgiving Day is the fourth Thursday in November, but is often the principal theme of the preceding Sunday. Thus specific decisions regarding both the day and the style of celebration are involved in any given year. The orders of service with brief commentaries which follow are designed with flexibility and local adaptability in mind. Many churches already have a tradition of ecumenical gatherings for Thanksgiving Day itself. In such a case, designating the last Sunday before Advent as the Feast of Christ the King is appropriate, and the order of service for Thanksgiving may be adapted to the needs of the particular worshiping community.

ALL SAINTS' DAY

GATHERING
Suitable festive music, choral or instrumental, may be offered during the gathering of the people.

GREETING
Grace to you and peace from God who is, and was, and is to come.
Amen.
And from Jesus Christ the faithful witness, the first-born of the dead, the ruler of kings on earth.
Amen.
The grace of the Lord Jesus be with all the saints.
Amen.

HYMN
"Rejoice, the Lord Is King," "All Praise to Our Redeeming Lord," "Come, Let Us Join Our Friends Above," "We Bear the Strain of Earthly Care," *and* "Through All the Changing Scenes of Life" *(BOH) are especially appropriate for beginning the service. If there is to be a procession or entrance song, it precedes the greeting. See Appendix 2 for other hymn suggestions.*

OPENING PRAYER
The Lord be with you.
And also with you.
Let us pray: *(a brief pause)*
God of all holiness,
   you gave our saints different gifts on earth
   but one holy city in heaven.
Give us grace to follow their good example,
   that we may know the joy you have prepared

for all who love you;
Through your Son Jesus Christ our Lord.
Amen.

or

Almighty God,
    you have knit together your elect
        into one communion and fellowship
    in the mystical body of your Son Christ our Lord:
Give us grace so to follow your blessed saints
    in all virtuous and godly living,
    that we may come to those ineffable joys
        which you have prepared
    for those who truly love you;
Through Jesus Christ our Lord,
    who with you and the Holy Spirit lives and reigns,
    one God, in glory everlasting.
Amen.

FIRST LESSON
    Revelation 7:9-17   (Year A: 1984, 1987)
    Revelation 21:1-6*a*   (Year B: 1985, 1988)
    Daniel 7:1-3, 15-18   (Year C: 1986, 1989)

PSALM (HYMN or ANTHEM)
    Psalm 34:1-10 or *BOH* 566   (Year A: 1984, 1987)
    Psalm 24:1-6 or *BOH* 561   (Year B: 1985, 1988)

Antiphon:
    **Rejoice you pure in heart! Rejoice,
        give thanks and sing.**

    The earth is the Lord's and all that is in it,
        the world and all who dwell therein.

    For it is God who founded it upon the seas
        and made it firm upon the rivers of the deep.

Antiphon:
    **Rejoice you pure in heart! Rejoice,
        give thanks and sing.**

Who can ascend the hill of the Lord?
and who can stand in God's holy place?

Those who have clean hands and a pure heart,
who have not pledged themselves to falsehood,
nor sworn by what is a fraud.

Antiphon:
**Rejoice you pure in heart! Rejoice,
give thanks and sing.**

They shall receive a blessing from the Lord and
a just reward from the God of their salvation.

Such is the generation of those who seek him,
of those who seek your face, O God of Jacob.

Antiphon:
**Rejoice you pure in heart! Rejoice,
give thanks and sing.**

Psalm 149 or *BOH* 556   (Year C: 1986, 1989)

SECOND LESSON
I John 3:1-3   (Year A: 1984, 1987)
Colossians 1:9-14   (Year B: 1985, 1988)
Ephesians 1:11-23   (Year C: 1986, 1989)

ALLELUIA (HYMN or ANTHEM)
"At the Name of Jesus," "Blest Are the Pure in Heart,"
or "Faith of Our Fathers" *(BOH)*.

GOSPEL
Matthew 5:1-12   (Year A: 1984, 1987)
John 11:32-44   (Year B: 1985, 1988)
Luke 6:20-36   (Year C: 1986, 1989)

SERMON

PRAYERS OF THE PEOPLE
*This may begin with a brief silence following a simple call to
prayer or the versicle and response:*

The Lord be with you.
And also with you.
Let us pray:
Holy God, we pray for your human family everywhere;
That we may be one.
Grant that all who are baptized into Christ may faithfully
    serve you;
That your name may be glorified on earth as in heaven.
We pray for all bishops, pastors, and deacons;
That there may be justice and peace on the earth.
Give us grace to do your will in all that we undertake;
That our works may find favor in your sight.
Have compassion on those who suffer from any grief or
    trouble;
That they may be delivered from their distress.
Give to the departed eternal rest;
Let light perpetual shine upon them.
We praise you for your saints who have entered into joy;
May we also come to share in your heavenly kingdom.
Let us pray for our own needs and those of others.

(silence)

*The people may add their petitions, following which the
presiding minister may add a suitable collect or other brief
concluding prayer.*

or

PRAYERS FOR THE SAINTS
AND THE FAITHFUL DEPARTED

*This is especially appropriate if the names of all persons in the
congregation who have died during the year are either read or
commemorated in some other way.*

O God of both the living and the dead,
    we praise your holy name for all your servants
      who have finished their course in faith,
    especially . . . *(here the names may be given).*

We pray that, encouraged by their example
    and strengthened by their fellowship,
    we may be partakers with them
    of the inheritance of the saints in light;
Through the merits of your Son Jesus Christ our Lord.
Amen.

or

PRAYER OF PRAISE FOR ALL THE SAINTS
    *(If the Lord's Supper is to be celebrated using the Great
    Thanksgiving, this prayer need not be included.)*

Blessed are you,
God of creation and of all beginnings,
God of Abraham and Sarah,
God of Miriam and Moses,
God of Joshua and Deborah,
God of Ruth and David,
God of the priests and the prophets,
God of Mary and Joseph,
God of apostles and martyrs,
God of our mothers and our fathers,
God of our children to all generations.

You made us in your image;
and though we all have sinned
and fallen short of your glory,
you loved the world so much
you gave your only Son Jesus Christ
to be our Savior.
Through his suffering and death,
his resurrection and ascension,
you gave birth to your Church,
delivered us from slavery to sin and death,
made with us a new covenant,
and baptized us with the Holy Spirit and with fire.

Therefore,
in remembrance of all your mighty acts in Jesus Christ,
we offer our lives in your service
as a living and holy surrender of ourselves.

Send the power of your Holy Spirit on us
that we may know the presence of the living Christ,
be one body in him,
and grow into his likeness.

Renew our communion with all your saints,
especially those whom we name before you
. . . [in our hearts].
May we run with perseverance
the race that is set before us,
being surrounded by so great a cloud of witnesses
and looking to Jesus,
the pioneer and perfecter of our faith,
and to his coming in final victory.

Through him, with him, in him,
in the unity of the Holy Spirit,
all honor and glory is yours,
Almighty God,
now and for ever.

Amen.

[THE PEACE]

OFFERING

A suitable anthem or instrumental music may be offered. If Holy Communion is to be celebrated, the gifts of bread and wine may be brought in procession along with the offering. One stanza of "Now Thank We All Our God" is a good alternative to the Doxology.

THE GREAT THANKSGIVING
The Lord be with you.
And also with you.

Lift up your hearts.
We lift them to the Lord.
Let us give thanks to the Lord our God.
It is right to give him thanks and praise.

Blessed are you, Almighty Father:
God of creation and of all beginnings,
God of Abraham and Sarah,
God of Miriam and Moses,
God of Joshua and Deborah,
God of Ruth and David,
God of the priests and the prophets,
God of Mary and Joseph,
God of apostles and martyrs,
God of our mothers and our fathers,
God of our children to all generations.

You made us in your image;
and though we all have sinned
and fallen short of your glory,
you loved the world so much
you gave your only Son Jesus Christ
to be our Savior.
Through his suffering and death,
his resurrection and ascension,
you gave birth to your Church,
delivered us from slavery to sin and death,
made with us a new covenant,
and baptized us with the Holy Spirit and with fire.

Therefore,
with your people in all ages
and the whole company of heaven,
we join in the song of unending praise,
singing (saying):

Holy, holy, holy Lord,
God of power and might,
heaven and earth are full of your glory.

Hosanna in the highest.
Blessed is he who comes in the name of the Lord.
Hosanna in the highest.

Truly holy are you,
and blessed is your Son Jesus Christ.
On the night he offered himself up for us
he took bread,
gave thanks to you,
broke the bread,
gave it to his disciples, and said:
"Take, eat;
this is my body which is given for you.
Do this in remembrance of me."

When the supper was over
he took the cup,
gave thanks to you,
gave it to his disciples, and said:
"Drink from this, all of you;
for this is my blood of the new covenant,
poured out for you and for many,
for the forgiveness of sins.
Do this, as often as you drink it,
in remembrance of me."

Therefore,
in remembrance of all your mighty acts in Jesus Christ,
we ask you to accept this
our sacrifice of praise and thanksgiving,
which we offer in union with Christ's sacrifice for us,
as a living and holy surrender of ourselves.

Send the power of your Holy Spirit on us
and on these gifts,
that in the breaking of this bread
and the drinking of this wine
we may know the presence of the living Christ,

be one body in him,
and grow into his likeness.

Renew our communion with all your saints,
especially those whom we name before you
. . . [in our hearts].

May we run with perseverance
the race that is set before us,
being surrounded by so great a cloud of witnesses
and looking to Jesus,
the pioneer and perfecter of our faith,
and to his coming
in final victory.

Through him, with him, in him,
in the unity of the Holy Spirit,
all honor and glory is yours,
Almighty Father,
now and for ever.

Amen.

THE LORD'S PRAYER

THE BREAKING OF THE BREAD

COMMUNION
Communion Hymns: "Come, Let Us Join Our Friends
Above," "How Happy Every Child of Grace," *or* "On
Jordan's Stormy Banks I Stand" *(BOH)*.

PRAYER AFTER COMMUNION
You have given yourself to us, Lord.
Now we give ourselves for others.
Your love has made us a new people.
As a people of love we will serve you with joy.
Your glory has filled our hearts.
Help us to glorify you in all things.
Amen.

HYMN
"For All the Saints," *or* "How Firm a Foundation" *(BOH)*

DISMISSAL WITH BLESSING

Go in peace to serve God and your neighbor
in all that you do.

We are sent in Christ's name.

The grace of the Lord Jesus Christ
and the love of God
and the communion of the Holy Spirit
be with you all.

(II Corinthians 13:14)

Amen.

or

Now unto him that is able to keep you from falling,
and to present you faultless
    before the presence
of his glory with exceeding joy:
to the only wise God our Savior,
be glory and majesty,
dominion and power,
both now and for ever.

(Jude 24-25)

Amen.
Let us bless the Lord.
Thanks be to God.

In planning for the celebration of All Saints' Day,
whether on November 1, or on the first Sunday of
November, we must take several factors into considera-
tion. What are the basic biblical and theological themes
and images that are being proclaimed and expressed?
What experience of faith does this particular congregation
have with the "communion of saints"—the solidarity of
the living and the dead in Jesus Christ? Who are the
examples of faith—people who have "walked with God"

in the history of Christianity, and in this particular church—people who are sources of encouragement and holiness to us? What are the particular gifts and resources of this local church, and what are the possibilities and restrictions in the particular sanctuary and/or related spaces in which this service will take place? What style of music and congregational participation will both reach people and enable them to participate deeply in the meaning of the service?

This should be a day of remembrance in which we encounter anew the most profound dimensions of what it is to be the Church. There is a clear eschatological vision and tone to this celebration, since it reminds us of those for whom the battle is over, the victory won, and also of our continuing pilgrimage toward God and the heavenly banquet. This is why the Lord's Supper should be celebrated with particular joy and solemnity. Time and again Wesley refers to All Saints' Day as a day of triumphant joy. As he remarks in his journal, "Nov. 1 was a day of triumphant joy, as All Saints' Day generally is. How superstitious are they who scruple giving God solemn thanks for the lives and deaths of his saints!" To render thanks to God for the lives and deaths of the saints is to recognize the common bond between the Church on earth and the Church triumphant in God's love. It is this vision that is so marvelously expressed in the Great Thanksgiving prayer at the table.

It might be possible in some circumstances to begin the service with a procession of the congregation or a representative group, along with the musicians and principal ministers. This could be done to the accompaniment of various kinds of instruments, depending upon what is available and appropriate. Care should be taken to choose music that does not trivialize the theme. On the other hand, a strong version of "When the Saints Go Marching In" may be done with great integrity and allow some spontaneous joy in the procession, with banners and/or signs with the names of saints. Brass and organ may be used to good effect. A charming hymn for use between lessons is "I Sing a Song of the Saints of God." This could be sung by a children's choir. *Seasons of the Gospel* gives some helpful suggestions on pages 107-8.

Particular groups within the congregation may wish to construct symbols of favorite saints to place at the entrance of the church or in the room of celebration. The tone of the whole service may reflect the solemnity of also remembering specific persons who have died, making this, in effect, a Christian Memorial Day. This needs to be approached with sensitivity and might best be incorporated into the Prayers of the People following the sermon. The preacher may find it appropriate to connect the Beatitudes with specific lives, in light of the Scripture lessons. In some circumstances it is possible to have a time of witnessing to the lives of the saints directly from the congregation, following the sermon. It is helpful to have one or two lay people give brief prepared testimonies as a model to others who may then be led to speak. This might also be correlated with particular traditional saints whose lives have influenced persons we have known who have encouraged us.

It is certainly possible to use a strong hymn such as "For All the Saints" as the opening hymn, while closing with the familiar "Blest Be the Tie That Binds," perhaps with the congregation joining hands. In this instance the second form of the Dismissal with Blessing might be used, followed by the exchange of the Peace (instead of earlier in the service). Or the final hymn might be a strong processional, once again with banners depicting individual saints, the cross, and the Bible. In this case the presiding minister would remain in front to give the Dismissal with Blessing, followed by a moment of silence and the postlude.

FEAST OF CHRIST THE KING

GATHERING

Festival music, based upon the hymn tunes, is particularly appropriate as the people gather. Symbols and/or banners of royalty may add a visual focus to the service and may be brought in procession if space and style permit.

GREETING

"I am the Alpha and the Omega," says the Lord God, who is, and was, and is to come, the Almighty.

Blessing and honor and glory and might be unto the Lamb!

Worthy is Christ who has ransomed us by his blood from every tribe and tongue and nation,

and made his people a kingdom, and priests to our God.

Holy, holy, holy is the Lord God Almighty,
who is, and was, and is to come!

HYMN

"Hail, Thou Once Despised Jesus," "The Head That Once Was Crowned," "Jesus Shall Reign," "O Worship the King," "O Thou Eternal Christ of God," "Christ Jesus Lay in Death's Strong Hands," "The Lord Will Come and Not Be Slow," "O Thou Who Art the Shepherd," *and* "At the Name of Jesus" *(BOH) are good opening hymns. If this is to be an entrance hymn with procession, it precedes the greeting.*

OPENING PRAYER

The Lord be with you.

And also with you.

Let us pray: *(a brief pause)*

All-powerful God,
    your only Son came to earth
    in the form of a slave

and is now enthroned at your right hand
  where he rules in glory.
As he reigns as King in our hearts,
  may we rejoice in his peace,
  glory in his justice,
  and live in his love.
For with you and the Holy Spirit
  he rules now and for ever.
Amen.

FIRST LESSON
  Ezekiel 34:11-16, 20-24   (Year A: 1984, 1987)
  Jeremiah 23:1-6   (Year B: 1985, 1988)
  II Samuel 5:1-5   (Year C: 1986, 1989)

PSALM (HYMN or ANTHEM)
  Psalm 23 or *BOH* 560   (Year A: 1984, 1987)
  Psalm 93 or *BOH* 582   (Year B: 1985, 1988)
  Psalm 95 or *BOH* 582   (Year C: 1986, 1989)

SECOND LESSON
  I Corinthians 15:20-28   (Year A: 1984, 1987)
  Revelation 1:4*b*-8   (Year B: 1985, 1988)
  Colossians 1:11-20   (Year C: 1986, 1989)

ALLELUIA (HYMN or ANTHEM)

GOSPEL
  Matthew 25:31-46   (Year A: 1984, 1987)
  John 18:33-37   (Year B: 1985, 1988)
  John 12:9-19   (Year C: 1986, 1989)

SERMON

[CREED]
  (especially if the Lord's Supper is not celebrated)

PRAYERS OF THE PEOPLE or PASTORAL PRAYER
  To each petition the people may respond:
  By the mercies of Christ, hear us.

THE LORD'S PRAYER
(if the Lord's Supper is not celebrated)
Introduced by a suitable phrase such as:
Let us pray for the Kingdom in the words Jesus gave us.

OFFERING
Suitable choral or instrumental music. The gifts may be presented while one or two stanzas of a Christ-centered hymn ("Rejoice, the Lord Is King," "Lead On, O King Eternal," stanza 4, or "Lord, Whose Love Through Humble Service," stanza 1 [BOH]) are sung. The Offering may precede the Prayers if Communion is not celebrated, followed by the concluding hymn with blessing and dismissal. If Communion is celebrated, the gifts of bread and wine may be brought forward in procession, and the people then remain standing for the Great Thanksgiving.

THE GREAT THANKSGIVING
The section within brackets is especially appropriate when reference is being made to responsibility for justice, peace, and to the nation being under the rule of Christ. At other times the section may be omitted.
The Lord be with you.
And also with you.
Lift up your hearts.
We lift them to the Lord.
Let us give thanks to the Lord our God.
It is right to give him thanks and praise.
Blessed are you, Lord our God,
Creator and Sovereign of the universe.
It is fitting that we give you thanks and praise.

[You created a land rich in resources
and set before the founders and pioneers
of our nation
an opportunity beyond measure

to build a realm of justice, peace, and freedom
that might be a blessing to all the world.

Even when we have abused your land
and turned aside from your ways,
you have been slow to anger
and abounding in mercy.
Through many voices
you have called us back to your way
and nurtured in our hearts a noble dream.]

Therefore,
with your people in every nation and in all ages
and the whole company of heaven,
we join in the song of unending praise,
singing (saying):

Holy, holy, holy Lord,
God of power and might,
heaven and earth are full of your glory.
Hosanna in the highest.
Blessed is he who comes in the name of the Lord.
Hosanna in the highest.

Truly holy are you,
and blessed is your Son Jesus Christ.
In the fullness of time you gave him
to be for us the way, the truth, and the life.
He proclaimed justice to all peoples
and brought good news to the poor,
release to the captives,
sight to the blind,
and freedom to the oppressed.
He healed the sick, fed the hungry,
and ate with those whom others scorned.

On the night his disciples betrayed and deserted him
he took bread,
gave thanks to you,

broke the bread,
gave it to his disciples, and said:
"Take, eat;
this is my body which is given for you.
Do this in remembrance of me."

When the supper was over
he took the cup,
gave thanks to you,
gave it to his disciples, and said:
"Drink from this, all of you;
for this is my blood of the new covenant,
poured out for you and for many,
for the forgiveness of sins.
Do this, as often as you drink it,
in remembrance of me."

By his death and resurrection
he delivered us from slavery to sin and death
and won for you a new people
by water and the Spirit.
At his ascension you exalted him
to sit and reign with you at your right hand.
We his people have beheld his glory,
and we acknowledge him to be our King.

Therefore,
in remembrance of all your mighty acts in Jesus Christ,
we ask you to accept this
our pledge of allegiance to him and to his kingdom,
in union with Christ's pledge of eternal love for us,
sealed with his blood.

Send the power of your Holy Spirit on us
and on these gifts,
that in the breaking of this bread
and the drinking of this wine
we may know the presence of the living Christ;
be one body in him, cleansed by his blood;

faithfully serve him in our nation and in the world;
and look forward to his coming
in final victory.

Hasten the day
when the prophets' dream shall come to pass,
when justice shall roll down like waters
and righteousness like an ever-flowing stream,
when nation shall not lift up sword against nation,
neither shall they learn war any more.

Through your Son Jesus Christ
with the Holy Spirit
in your holy Church,
all glory and honor is yours,
Almighty God,
now and for ever.
Amen.

THE BREAKING OF THE BREAD

COMMUNION
Appropriate hymns: "Jesus, We Look to Thee," "Jesus,
with Thy Church Abide," "Be Known to Us in Breaking
Bread," "Bread of the World," "O the Depth of Love
Divine" *(BOH);* "As We Break the Bread," "Cup of
Blessing That We Share," "I Come with Joy" *(SBH).*

PRAYER AFTER COMMUNION
You have given yourself to us, Lord.
Now we give ourselves for others.
Your love has made us a new people.
As a people of love we will serve you with joy.
Your glory has filled our hearts.
Help us to glorify you in all things.
Amen.

HYMN
"Jesus Shall Reign," "Rejoice, the Lord Is King" *(BOH);*

"O Jesus Christ, to You May Hymns," "When the Church of Jesus" *(SBH);* "Soon and Very Soon" *(SZ).*

DISMISSAL WITH BLESSING

May God who is, and was, and is to come, bless you and keep you.
Amen.
May Jesus Christ, the faithful witness
and ruler of all nations,
make his face to shine upon you.
Amen.
May the Holy Spirit, who guides us into all truth,
grant you peace.
Amen.
Go in the strong name of Jesus Christ.
Thanks be to God!

This final Sunday of the Season After Pentecost is the Sunday before Advent. If services are not held on Thanksgiving Day, the Feast of Christ the King will often coincide with Thanksgiving Sunday. The Gospel readings from God's Word according to the lectionary have concentrated upon the teachings of Jesus and often contain parables about the kingdom. Therefore it is appropriate to celebrate the rule of Christ, who, in the lineage of David, is both Shepherd and Ruler of all. This day presents the opportunity to preach on Jesus as the crucified King, now seated upon the throne and blessing the whole world.

While the themes of Thanksgiving and the rule of Christ may be seen in light of each other, care must be taken in planning the particular character of this service. The worship committee may wish to study the Great Thanksgiving, which may be used for either occasion, to assist in the selection of hymns, prayers, choral music, and related visuals if the service is to combine the themes. A study of the themes of the lections in the appropriate year will show various prefigurations of Christ's rule in the Old Testament reading, a particular unfolding of the meaning of the messianic age in the Epistle, and a portrayal of the paradox: servant/king. Pastors may find helpful insights in *Social Themes of the Christian Year: A Commentary on the Lectionary,* edited by Dieter T. Hessel (Philadelphia: The Geneva Press, 1983).

Musical variations will give particular emphasis to the service. For example, "Soon and Very Soon" from *Songs of Zion* may be used between the Epistle and Gospel readings, or as a response to the offering. A powerful congregational response, which may be extended as a prayerful ending to the intercessions, pastoral prayer, or Communion, "Jesus, Remember Me," is found in *Music from Taize* by Jacques Berthier (Chicago: G.I.A. Publications, 1981).

THANKSGIVING DAY

GATHERING

Suitable choral or instrumental music may be offered as the people gather. Congregational singing of hymns of thanksgiving may provide an alternative in some circumstances. If this is an ecumenical gathering, hymns or songs from the various traditions represented may be sung.

GREETING

Let the nations be glad and sing for joy,
for you judge the peoples with equity
and guide all the nations upon.earth.
Let all the peoples praise you, O God;
let all the peoples praise you.
The earth has brought forth her increase;
may God, our own God, give us his blessing.

Let all the peoples praise you, O God;
let all the peoples praise you.

HYMN

"Come, Ye Thankful People, Come," "All People That
on Earth Do Dwell," "Now Thank We All Our God,"
"Praise to the Lord, the Almighty," "We Plow the
Fields," "O God, Thou Giver of All Good" *(BOH);* "O
Jesus Christ, to You May Hymns," *and* "O Love, How
Deep" *(SBH) are especially appropriate for the entrance hymn
or processional. See also the section under "Thanksgiving" in
the topical index (BOH 851). The greeting will follow the hymn
if there is a processional with banners, cross, and Bible.*

OPENING PRAYER

The Lord be with you.
And also with you.
Let us pray: *(a brief pause)*
Lord our God,
Love began with you
    and has filled our cup to overflowing.
In the abundance of your countless gifts,
    give us your grace to fill others' lives with love,
    that we may be more nearly worthy
    of all you have given us.
We ask this in the name of Jesus the Lord.
Amen.

or

Almighty and gracious Father,
    we give you thanks
for the fruits of the earth in their season
    and for the labors of those who harvest them.
Make us, we pray,
    faithful stewards of your great bounty,
    for the provision for our necessities,
    and for the relief of all who are in need,

to the glory of your name;
Through Jesus Christ our Lord,
    who lives and reigns with you and the Holy Spirit,
    one God, now and for ever.
Amen.

or

*If a prayer of confession is desired, the minister may address the
people:*
Dear friends in Christ, aware of God's providence and
grace, let us bow in silence before God to confess our
sins and obtain forgiveness: *(a brief pause)*
Most merciful God,
    we confess that we have sinned against you
    in thought, word, and deed.
We have not loved you with our whole heart;
    we have not loved our neighbors as ourselves.
We pray you: in your mercy
    forgive what we have been,
    amend what we are,
    direct what we shall be;
    that we may delight in your will
    and walk in your ways,
    giving thanks in all circumstances
    through Jesus Christ our Lord. Amen.
Friends, hear the good news:
In the name of Jesus Christ, you are forgiven!
In the name of Jesus Christ, you are forgiven!
Glory to God. Amen.

[ACT OF PRAISE]
*Here may be sung the "Gloria Patri," the "Jubilate Deo," or
the "Te Deum" (BOH 669 and 665), or a choral setting of
these or similar canticles may be sung by the choir.*

FIRST LESSON
    Deuteronomy 8:7-18   (Year A: 1984, 1987)

Joel 2:21-27   (Year B: 1985, 1988)
Deuteronomy 26:1-11   (Year C: 1986, 1989)

PSALM (HYMN or ANTHEM)
Psalm 65   (Year A: 1984, 1987)
Psalm 126   (Year B: 1985, 1988)

Antiphon:
Praise and thanks to you, O God in Zion!
You visit the earth and water it abundantly.
You make it very plenteous;
    the river of God is full of water.
You prepare the grain,
    for so you provide for the earth.
You drench the furrows and smooth out the ridges;
    with heavy rain you soften the ground
    and bless its increase.
You crown the year with your goodness,
    and your paths overflow with plenty.
May the fields of the wilderness be rich for grazing,
    and the hills be clothed with joy.
May the meadows cover themselves with flocks,
    and the valleys cloak themselves with grain;
    let them shout for joy and sing.

Antiphon:
Praise and thanks to you, O God in Zion!
Psalm 100   (Year C: 1986, 1989)

SECOND LESSON
II Corinthians 9:6-15   (Year A: 1984, 1987)
I Timothy 2:1-7   (Year B: 1985, 1988)
Philippians 4:4-9   (Year C: 1986, 1989)

ALLELUIA (HYMN or ANTHEM)

GOSPEL
Luke 17:11-19   (Year A: 1984, 1987)
Matthew 6:25-33   (Year B: 1985, 1988)
John 6:15-35   (Year C: 1986, 1989)

SERMON

PRAYERS OF THE PEOPLE or PASTORAL PRAYER

If a special offering of food is to be brought by the people in procession or by representatives, these prayers or the Litany of Thanksgiving may follow the offertory. If the people make their own petitions, the common response to each may be: **Most gracious God, hear our prayer.**

or

A LITANY OF THANKSGIVING *(see Appendix 1)*

[THE PEACE]

All may exchange signs of reconciliation and peace silently, or with the traditional **The peace of the Lord be with you.**

OFFERING

A suitable anthem or instrumental music may be offered. If Holy Communion is to be celebrated, the gifts of bread and wine may be brought in procession with the offering (in concluding a procession of food gifts—see commentary). If Holy Communion is not celebrated, the service concludes with a hymn, blessing, and dismissal.

OFFERTORY SONG

(as alternative to Doxology) "We Give Thee But Thine Own," *stanza 1 (BOH).*

or

Father, Son, and Holy Ghost,
    One in Three, and Three in One,
As by the celestial host
    Let Thy will on earth by done;
Praise by all to Thee be given,
    Gracious Lord of earth and heaven!

•   •   •

Take my soul and body's powers,
    Take my memory, mind, and will,

All my goods, and all my hours,
  All I know, and all I feel,
All I think, and speak, and do;
  Take my heart—but make it new.
Charles Wesley

THE GREAT THANKSGIVING
  The Lord be with you.
  And also with you.
  Lift up your hearts.
  We lift them to the Lord.
  Let us give thanks to the Lord our God.
  It is right to give him thanks and praise.
  Blessed are you, Lord our God,
  Creator and Sovereign of the universe.
  You call the worlds into being,
  and by your appointment the seasons come and go.
  You bring forth bread from the earth
  and create the fruit of the vine.
  You have made us in your image
  and given us dominion over the world.
  Earth has yielded its treasure,
  and from your hand
  we have received blessing on blessing.

  Therefore,
  with your people in all ages
  and the whole company of heaven,
  we join in the song of unending praise,
  singing (saying):
  Holy, holy, holy Lord,
  God of power and might,
  heaven and earth are full of your glory.
  Hosanna in the highest.
  Blessed is he
  who comes in the name of the Lord.
  Hosanna in the highest.

Holy Father,
we bless you for your boundless love
in the redemption of the world
by your Son Jesus Christ.
Though he was rich,
yet for our sake he became poor.
When he was hungry,
he resisted the temptation to make bread for himself,
that he might be the bread of life for others.
When the multitudes were hungry,
he fed them.
He broke bread with those whom others scorned,
but the greedy he drove out of the Temple.
On the night he offered himself up for us
he took bread,
gave thanks to you,
broke the bread,
gave it to his disciples, and said:
"Take, eat;
this is my body which is given for you.
Do this in remembrance of me."

When the supper was over
he took the cup,
gave thanks to you,
gave it to his disciples, and said:
"Drink from this, all of you;
for this is my blood of the new covenant,
poured out for you and for many,
for the forgiveness of sins.
Do this, as often as you drink it,
in remembrance of me."

On the day you raised him from the dead
he was recognized by his disciples
in the breaking of the bread,
and as he continued to appear in their midst

he ate in their presence and gave them food.
In the power of your Holy Spirit
your Church has continued
in the breaking of bread
and the sharing of the cup.

Therefore,
recalling your Son's death and resurrection,
his ascension and his abiding presence
through your Holy Spirit,
we ask you to accept this
our sacrifice of praise and thanksgiving,
which we offer in union with Christ's sacrifice for us,
as a living and holy surrender of ourselves.

Send the power of your Holy Spirit on us
and on these gifts of bread and wine,
that in the breaking of this bread
and the drinking of this wine
we may know the presence of the living Christ;
be one body in him, cleansed by his blood;
faithfully serve him in the world;
and look forward to his coming
in final victory.
Through him, with him, in him,
in the unity of the Holy Spirit,
all honor and glory is yours,
Almighty Father,
now and for ever.
Amen.

THE LORD'S PRAYER

THE BREAKING OF THE BREAD

COMMUNION
*Hymns or psalms may be sung during the Communion, or a
suitable anthem may be offered toward the end of the people's*

sharing, perhaps followed by a brief silence in meditative response.

PRAYER AFTER COMMUNION

You have given yourself to us, Lord;
Now we give ourselves for others.
Your love has made us a new people;
As a people of love we will serve you with joy.
Your glory has filled our hearts;
Help us to glorify you in all things.

or

Eternal God, heavenly Father,
 you have graciously accepted us as living members
 of your Son our Savior Jesus Christ,
 and you have fed us with spiritual food
 in the Sacrament of his Body and Blood.
Send us now into the world in peace,
 and grant us strength and courage
 to love and serve you
 with gladness and singleness of heart;
 through Christ our Lord.
Amen.

HYMN

Depending upon the theme of the sermon and the specific tone of the service, the following hymns are appropriate: "Now Thank We All Our God," "Lord, Whose Love Through Humble Service," "O God, Thou Giver of All Good," "Not Alone for Mighty Empire" *(BOH).*

DISMISSAL WITH BLESSING

Go in peace to love and serve the Lord.
Thanks be to God.
The grace of the Lord Jesus Christ
 and the love of God
 and the fellowship of the Holy Spirit
 be with you all, now and for ever.
Amen.

Thanksgiving presents us with a number of possibilities. If it is celebrated on Thursday, it may be a gathering of several churches for an ecumenical service. Such an occasion provides an excellent opportunity for shared ministry among choirs and worship leaders from the various traditions, and especially for congregational singing of hymns and songs from the respective churches. This would be an equally appropriate occasion to use music from ethnic and minority traditions, both choral and congregational. *Songs of Zion* (SWR 12) provides one such excellent resource; it includes, among others, "Lift Every Voice and Sing." *Hymns from the Four Winds, Ecumenical Praise*, and *The Supplement to The Book of Hymns* should be used in planning the service.

An alternative approach to the reading and proclamation of Scripture is to correlate readings with hymns and/or anthems interspersed. If there are several choirs involved, the sermon might be shortened appropriately. In this case the accent falls on praise and thanks. The Litany of Thanksgiving provided may be the central congregational act following the sermon. Another form of thanksgiving prayer, if Holy Communion is not celebrated, is the Great Thanksgiving in *At the Lord's Table* (#19 or #20), used without the lines which have a vertical rule beside them—that is, omitting the institutional narrative "On the night . . ." and the calling of the Holy Spirit upon the gifts of bread and wine.

Thanksgiving presents an especially appropriate occasion for an ecumenical sharing in the Lord's Supper as well. Special care must be taken in preparation to be sensitive to the various traditions represented, as well as to the possibilities of space and the manner of communing. Special banners which could be used from year to year are to be encouraged; and the concept of a community offering of gifts of food for the needy, or for a particular agency of relief, may be a powerful expression of our Christian response and responsibility to the heritage of Thanksgiving. Intercessory prayers of petition may be for the specific persons or agencies for whom the gifts are intended. The gifts themselves may be brought to a designated place near the altar as the people gather, or a representative gift may be brought forward with the gifts of bread and wine; or, if the Eucharist is not celebrated, the food gifts may be brought to the altar with the offering.

If the service takes place on the Sunday prior to Thanksgiving, such a special offering is strongly recommended. The pastor and the planning committee may wish to emphasize Christian responsibility more explicitly by using Great Thanksgiving "The Gift of Food" (#19) for the Holy Communion, or adapt it for the prayer following the sermon and offering, the appropriate lines being omitted.

ADVENT, CHRISTMAS, AND THE EPIPHANY:

A Theological and Historical Introduction

Christians confess and proclaim that "the Word became flesh and dwelt among us" (John 1:14). This is the great message of the Incarnation—that Jesus Christ was born into human history in the fullness of time for the salvation of the world. We seek to celebrate, to proclaim, and to manifest this message to all peoples in this particular season of the Church's year of grace.

During Advent, we sing "Come, thou long-expected Jesus, / Born to set thy people free." At Christmas we join with the herald angels, singing "Glory to the new-born King!" The Epiphany bids us behold the light shining in the darkness, the Root of Jesse, David's Son, to whom in adoration we sing, "O Morning Star, how fair and bright / Thou beamest forth in truth and light!" The story this season has to tell upon the mountain is one of "good tidings and great joy"—for the Messiah has come. Yet such is God's advent among us that we can never fully grasp the mystery of Incarnate Deity, so we must continue to remember and to experience anew, year upon year, the permanent crisis of light in the midst of the world's darkness and turmoil. We relive the fear and hope and joy which Christian worship expresses in the narrative of Christ's coming to judge the world in the form of an infant—the wood of whose cradle foreshadowed the cross.

The theology of Advent, Christmas, and the Epiphany is powerful because we cannot fully understand Jesus' birth without first understanding that he is Savior and Lord. This means that any authentic celebration of Advent and Christmas must be experienced as part of the larger story of his life, suffering, death, and resurrection. In other words, Incarnation is one central aspect of what, in *From Ashes to Fire*, we call the Paschal Mystery. The birth narratives in Matthew are themselves an expression of a saving faith in Christ. The worship patterns offered here will serve to heighten this inner connection between Christ's birth and his redemptive passion, death, and resurrection.

Christmas is, in many respects, more popular with Western Christians than is any other season of the year. The Eastern churches have, from the beginning, focused upon the Epiphany. Hispanic traditions have vividly portrayed the Three Kings. While there are certainly cultural reasons for these interests, the fundamental Western images and themes of Christmas seem more intimate and perhaps closer to the tenderness at the heart of humanity. Images of the Holy Family, the poverty and difficulty of their circumstances, the affectionate simplicity of the scenes at the manger, and the doxology on the starlit hillside—all combine to form a deep place of receptivity in the human heart for the news that heaven and earth have met, that God and humankind are reconciled. Certainly the innocence of the child and the dramatic swirl of events in Bethlehem and Jerusalem serve to capture our imagination. Various traditions have focused much devotional life around the crèche.

The Advent-Christmas-Epiphany cycle is both narrative and thematic, historical and theological. On one level it leads us through the narrative of hope and expectation for the coming Messiah expressed so powerfully by the prophets, especially Isaiah. Then Christmas and Epiphany take us from the birth narratives to the first manifestation of Jesus' identity and divinity in the gifts of the Magi, his baptism by John in the Jordan, and his first miracle at the wedding in Cana. At the same time, we are celebrating and proclaiming more than a simple chronology of events. The whole cycle also speaks of the yearning and hope of human beings for salvation, the wonder at God assuming human flesh, the wise men's anticipation of Jesus' death and burial, and the solidarity with humanity that is the very way of Emmanuel, God-with-us.

Thus to celebrate the Advent-Christmas-Epiphany cycle well, we must submit to its wide range of themes and emotions: from hope to joy, from darkness to light, from yearning for deliverance to the very manifestation of God's coming in judgment and in life-giving solidarity with humanity. There is a vision in the readings of redeemed society and an urgent expectancy of God's final shalom— justice, peace, righteousness, and reconciliation.

Historically, the special day in this whole cycle was originally the Epiphany. This day of "theophany," or manifestation of God's light and power in Christ, was, in addition to Easter and Pentecost, the third chief event in the Christian calendar of the early church. While its origins are not as clear as are those of Easter and Pentecost, its date, January 6, probably was the Christian substitute for the pagan feast celebrated in Egypt at the winter solstice. Thus the Epiphany speaks, in part, to the archetypal human experience of longing for light in the midst of the shortest and darkest days of the year.

It is clear from the earliest lectionaries and sermons,

however, that the Epiphany focused upon John 1:1–2:11. The themes, from its beginning, included Christ as light, his advent into the world, his baptism in the Jordan, and the first miracle of turning water into wine. Common to all these is the theological claim that God was in Jesus Christ, being manifest to human beings even to the ends of the earth.

In the fourth century, most probably in Rome, this unitary feast was divided, and what we now call Christmas emerged. The earliest account of this is from A.D. 354 and reflects the customs of the preceding generation. Christmas came to focus more exclusively than did the Epiphany upon the birth narratives and became much more prominent in the Western church. We have inherited a tendency to regard Christmas as emphasizing the Incarnation in a narrower sense than is appropriate to the full richness of Word made flesh and manifest in Jesus Christ.

In this book we stress the recovered balance of these themes with the Epiphany. For it is the more ancient of the two, and it includes a much richer theological set of meanings: the whole purpose and power of the Incarnation shown in the beginning of Jesus' ministry.

Advent also emerged early, as a season of preparation for the Epiphany. In A.D. 380 a council in Spain decreed that "from December 17 until the day of Epiphany [January 6] no one is permitted to be absent from Church." This indicates Advent's importance in the worship life of the Christians in Gaul. By the fifth century it had developed into a forty-day (adopting the biblical number) season of preparation. Rome and the Western churches declared it to be a four-week season before Christmas. For further historical details you may wish to consult *Seasons of the Gospel*, chapter 2, and James F. White's *Introduction to Christian Worship* (Abingdon Press, 1980), pp. 44-75.

The Gospel in Advent-Christmas-Epiphany

Advent is a season of great tension. It is primarily concerned with eschatology and not, as our contemporary American commercial sense would have it, with preparing for Christmas cheer. Instead, Advent expresses hope and expectation for both the first *and* the second coming of Christ. There is a paradox here. We designate the first Sunday of Advent as the beginning of the church year. Yet it plunges us immediately into the tension between the "already" of Christ having come in the flesh and the "not yet" of the consummation of all things in Christ at the end of time. Advent challenges us to rethink and confront, in Word and sacramental sign-acts, the revelation of Christ's time in the midst of our times. Thus we *begin* the year reflecting and praying together about the end of all history.

Seasons of the Gospel puts the point well: "Advent is both a time of thanks for the gift of Christ to us in past time and anticipation of his second coming. It contains both threat and promise" (p. 30). This characteristic of threat and promise is carried out in the lections and in the hymnody of the season, and thus we find a particular emphasis upon Advent hymns throughout the season, in distinction from Christmas carols and hymns. Generally speaking, most congregations have not received much exposure to or teaching in the range of texts such as "Lo, He Comes with Clouds Descending" or "There's a Voice in the Wilderness Crying." A study of the classical collects for each Sunday (Appendix 1) will disclose the theology of Advent in vivid images.

In planning services of worship during Advent, then, we must acknowledge that the readings express not merely expectation of Christ's nativity which has already happened, but the coming of Christ to rule, to judge, and to save. The hope in which the church participates and the expectation we share is of the kingdom come. In this sense the eschatological cry of our Lord's prayer is surely in tune with Advent: "Thy Kingdom come, thy will be done on earth . . ." Preaching is an exciting challenge in light of the lessons. The prophetic element is particularly strong throughout these Sundays: We hope for the destruction of the powers of evil, for the righteousness and justice of God, for the dawning of God's shalom over all the nations, and the undoing of the machines of war. For Christians this hope has been intensified by the first coming of Christ. Thus our preaching, praying, singing, and celebrating of the Gospel in these weeks should not be deprived of such rich and powerful eschatology. Only by experiencing these tensions, and the expectations of the whole groaning world in travail, can our participation in the dying and rising of Christ be made real. As Louis Bouyer has remarked, "The purpose of Advent, Christmas and Epiphany is ceaselessly to reanimate in us that hope, that expectation" (*Liturgical Piety*, p. 204).

This sheds new light on our celebration of Christmas and its immediately following days. For Christmas is far richer and deeper than a sentimental remembrance of the birth and childhood of Jesus. We should never deny nor suppress the intimacy and tenderness of the beginning point of Incarnation, but Christmas itself means much more. "Joy to the World, the Lord Is Come!" means precisely that the One who comes is indeed our Redeemer—the very One into whose dying and rising we are baptized, just as he was baptized into our human lot in the Jordan. If we understand Christmas in this way, our services will be capable of addressing the deepest human needs and touching our most profound experiences. This is why we must bring together resources for significant family worship, while at the same time we explore in new ways the larger repertoire of song, as with the Service of Lessons and Carols.

It is significant that the period between Christmas and the Epiphany became, for certain segments of the early church, a baptismal period second in importance only to the Easter Vigil and the Great Fifty Days (see *From Ashes to Fire*). The season of Christmas contains no mere secular sentiment; rather, it takes us through the witness of several martyrs and saints: December 26, Stephen, Deacon and Martyr; December 27, John, Apostle and Martyr; December 28, The Holy Innocents, martyrs; and January 1, the Name of Jesus and/or the Solemnity of Mary. While many Protestants have not observed these feasts, they serve to remind us of the powerful connection between Christmas and the Epiphany, and the baptismal reality of dying and rising with Christ.

The resources in this book place particular emphasis upon the possibilities of baptism and/or baptismal renewal during this season. John Wesley's Covenant Service, which has a venerable history of use on New Year's Eve as a Watch Night service, is also very suitable as a full congregational act on the Sunday called the Baptism of the Lord—the first Sunday following the Epiphany. Local pastors and congregations will certainly wish to explore the possibilities of baptismal celebrations as part of the regular services between Christmas and the Epiphany, with the explicit inclusion of the renewal of baptismal vows on the part of the whole congregation (see *A Service of Baptism, Confirmation, and Renewal*, rev. ed. 1980, SWR 2).

We can approach the Christmas-Epiphany season with a sense of excitement when we understand how the whole season initiates us into the manifestation of God in Jesus Christ. The Sundays following the Epiphany take us from Christ's own baptism through the signs and teachings and wonders he performed in his earthly ministry. It is as though the Epiphany and the whole season thereafter resound with the theme in John's Gospel: "The light shines in the darkness and the darkness has not overcome it." We behold Christ's glory in what he said and did—for we believe he says and does these very things in our day. The last Sunday after the Epiphany and before the beginning of Lent celebrates The Transfiguration of the Lord, a time filled with his glory in anticipation of the resurrected glory yet to come.

PREPARING THE PEOPLE AND THE PLACE:
Some Pastoral Suggestions

The Advent-Christmas-Epiphany cycle of the church year is an extraordinarily rich period. It presents Christians with a marvelous array of family and church customs and calls us to a deeper spiritual life together in Christ. At the same time, this season challenges us to create an environment of prayer and song, of Scripture, fellowship, and sacramental action to counter the crass commercialism which makes use of carols from Thanksgiving through Christmas, to sell anything and everything. Planning for Advent and Christmas-Epiphany requires a conviction as to the theological realities we are called to rediscover and to celebrate. To observe these days together, we must make decisions about the meaning that should be expressed by specific events, activities, and particular worship occasions, and about how the church as a whole community should prepare itself to enter into the rhythms and themes of Advent and Christmas-Epiphany. The following practical suggestions assume the reader's familiarity with chapter 2 of *From Ashes to Fire* and seek to provide help with specific features of the season at hand.

Advent Signs and Symbols

One of the most widespread and popular customs in churches and in homes during this season is the Advent wreath. For many congregations this may be one of the most visible signs, along with the change to purple or deep-blue paraments, of the first Sundays of the church year. The Advent wreath, which is traditionally suspended from the ceiling or an arch so as to suggest the shape of a tree, consists of four candles and a larger Christ-candle in the center. In many cases three of the candles are purple or dark blue and the fourth is rose, symbolizing the third Sunday of Advent (*gaudate*—"joy"). The actual color is not crucial, though we recommend that three of the candles be the same color, and the four smaller candles be the same size.

A candle is lighted on the first Sunday of Advent, usually during the very first part of the service, by a family or specially chosen layperson. One more is lighted each week until, on the fourth Sunday, all four are lighted. Finally on Christmas Eve or during the first service of Christmas Day, the middle white candle is lighted also.

There are several possibilities for this ceremony. Immediately following the opening hymn and collect, one member of the designated family may light the candle(s) while one or more other members recite or read an appropriate text:

First Sunday:
> We light this candle as a symbol of expectation. May the light sent from God shine in the darkness to show us the way to salvation. O come, O come Emmanuel!

Second Sunday:
> We light this candle as a symbol of hope. May the Word sent from God through the prophets lead us to the way of salvation. O come, O come Emmanuel!

Third Sunday:

We light this candle as a symbol of joy. May the joyful promise of your presence, O God, make us rejoice in our hope of salvation. O come, O come Emmanuel!

Fourth Sunday:

We light this candle as a symbol of purity. May the visitation of your Holy Spirit, O God, purify us that we may be ready for the coming of Jesus, our hope and joy. O come, O come Emmanuel!

Then on Christmas Eve or Christmas morning during the opening hymn or procession, the acolytes or other ministers may light all the candles, including the Christ candle.

Or the pattern of the O Antiphons could be used (see Appendix 1), reading a different one each Sunday, with the congregation and choir singing the refrain as their response to the lighting of the candle(s). The ceremony is performed by the designated persons immediately following the opening prayer or collect. The text is recited while the candle(s) are being lighted.

First Sunday:

O come, O come Emmanuel;
And ransom captive Israel;
That mourns in lonely exile here;
Until the Son of God appear;

(refrain)
Rejoice, Rejoice, Emmanuel shall come to thee, O Israel!

Second Sunday:

O come, thou Wisdom from on high;
Who orders all things mightily;
To us the path of knowledge show;
And teach us in its ways to go.
(refrain)

Third Sunday:

O come, thou Day-spring from on high;
And cheer us by thy drawing nigh;
Disperse the gloomy clouds of night;
And death's dark shadow put to flight.

(refrain)

Fourth Sunday:

O come, Desire of nations, bind;
In one the hearts of all humankind;
Bid thou our sad divisions cease;
And be thyself our King of Peace.

(refrain)

In a similar way, people in their homes may wish to have a brief reading or sing a stanza of a hymn to accompany the lighting of the various candles of the Advent wreath, which has been placed on a prominent table or in a central place. It would be especially appropriate to have this ceremony on Sundays or at evening meals during the week when the whole household is assembled. Each meal during the Christmas season would then witness the light of the Christ candle with a hymn and an opening table grace.

Nearly every local church and home will have a Christmas tree of some sort. The tradition of the Chrismon Tree is rapidly growing. This involves the use of various symbols from the genealogy of Christ and from his life, death, and resurrection. The tree is decorated during early Advent and stands as a reminder of the whole story and significance of Christ.

Christmas-tree customs have roots in the old mystery plays performed in churches as early as the eleventh century. From the so-called Paradise Play, we find the custom of the Paradise Tree. This represented the Garden of Eden, but also the tree of life and, by association, the tree upon which Christ was crucified for our redemption. Therefore the Paradise Tree contains various fruits: apples, oranges; small interestingly baked breads; pastry and candy.

Yet a third variation for church and home is sometimes referred to as the Jesse Tree and is basically a family tree of Jesus. The phrase of the prophet Isaiah, "A shoot will sprout from the stump of Jesse," gives us the image of this tree. As with the Chrismon Tree, various symbols that remind us of Christ's coming into human history are placed on the tree. Some figures are symbols of Christ from the Old Testament—Key of David, Scepter of Israel— while others represent various prophets and other figures in Scripture: Noah's ark, the tablets of the Law given to Moses, Abraham's knife, Jacob's ladder, the shell and sandals of John the Baptist, and so on.

Obviously the planning committee should choose one or another of these Advent tree customs.

The actual decoration of such trees may take place informally on Saturday or on a weekday evening. A brief service of prayer and song may precede, or better still, follow the decorating, along with festive refreshments. Or it could follow a Wednesday-night fellowship dinner, with all those attending being given a part in the tree ceremony. Careful planning is necessary if there are large numbers of people. The prayer service could use appropriate Scripture texts from which the various symbols are drawn. Suitable Advent hymns and carols may be sung.

The following poem, adapted from *Prayers, Poems and Songs* by Huub Oosterhuis, may be used as the whole group gathers about the tree:

> At last night is ending,
> the day is drawing near.

The people living in the night
will see the long-awaited light.
Rising in the darkness from afar,
it shines on them, the morning star.

The son of man will come once more,
not as a child, obscure and poor;
only the Father knows the day,
all we must do is watch and pray.

Though sun and moon may cease to shine,
we who believe will know his sign:
this is when we will understand
his second coming is at hand.

In the winter when the tree seems dead,
we have to hope and look ahead
to the green branch that will appear
when summer and new life are near.

Exposed to every wind and storm,
deprived of beauty and of form,
but we who live in faith know well
that branch is called Emmanuel.

God with us is a living name,
God will not put our faith to shame,
if we are open to receive
the Son in whom we all believe.

At last night is ending,
the day is drawing near.

The decorating of the tree and the placing of the Advent
wreath may also be incorporated into a regular Sunday
service. Have the tree set up, with the symbols already in
place on the top part of the tree. Then following the first
reading or a hymn, a procession may form and move to the

tree, where the symbols may be attached to the lower branches. The symbols may be placed beside the tree so that the people in the procession may pick them up, or they may be handed to the people one at a time as they reach the tree. In some local churches, it is possible to arrange the decorating prior to the morning service.

A related custom in many churches is the "hanging of the greens." Again, this may best be done following a weeknight supper. Depending upon the number of persons involved, the size of the room, and the extent of the greenery, this activity may be concluded with a short service of hymns or carols, Scripture readings, and prayer.

In an excellent resource titled *Keeping Advent* (rev. ed., 1975, The Liturgical Conference, 806 Rhode Island Avenue, NE, Washington DC 20018), the following paragraphs remind us of a special Advent gift a local church may give to others:

> Setting up a Jesse tree, Advent wreath, or paradise tree can become a part of a liturgy celebrated in a nursing home or home for retired citizens. Invite parishioners to come and worship at the local nursing home during Advent. It is a good time to bring the parish church to those unable to attend the worship center for services.
>
> During Advent, people everywhere will find themselves with much to do in the short space of time. Shopping, baking, decorating, praying, cleaning, all fill the weeks very easily. Christians need not reject these pre-Christmas activities, but should try to keep good perspective. Parishioners can be encouraged to bring gifts for the needy and place them around the tree of Jesse or paradise tree. These gifts can be distributed by volunteers.

Further care and planning for the Advent and Christmas environment should include the possibility of banners, textile art, and bulletins for the worship services (the covers and graphics and possibly text calligraphy). The biblical titles for Jesus in the Advent Antiphons, or those symbols used on the Chrismon or the Jesse Tree present a wide range of design. Simplicity and focus are desirable; clutter and busyness are not—especially during Advent. For example, simple and somber-hued bolts of cloth hung in bold verticals may be far more effective than wordy or cluttered banners. Use imagination and restraint: purple, blue, gray, and heavy textures are appropriate to Advent.

Then the transition to Christmas Eve or Christmas Day is striking: suddenly white, gold, yellow, with fine textures of cloth change the environment dramatically. Visual symbols for this season include angels, star bursts, shepherds, the manger, the Holy Family, and—above all—light and splendor. The Chrismon or the Jesse Tree provides continuity of symbolism against this changed visual background.

For the Epiphany, the environment should reflect visually the great images: the Magi; their gifts of gold, frankincense and myrrh; their three crowns. We may also use the imagery of the baptism in the Jordan; or the miracle at the wedding in Cana, with colorful earthen jugs representing water turned to wine.

// IV //

THE SUNDAYS OF ADVENT:
Alternative Orders of Worship

GATHERING
Suitable music, choral or instrumental, may be offered during the gathering of the people. If there is an organ, chorales of J. S. Bach from the Orgelbuchlein *are especially recommended. This music may be preceded by the decorating of the sanctuary, if appropriate.*

GREETING

#1
Show us your mercy, O Lord,
And grant us your salvation.
Truth shall spring up from the earth,
And righteousness shall look down from heaven.

or

#2
I will hear what the Lord God has to say.
A Voice that speaks for peace.
Peace for all people and for God's friends.
And to those who turn to God in their hearts.
Blessings on the One who comes in the name of the
  Lord.
Glory to God in the highest,
and peace to God's people on earth.

HYMN

"The King Shall Come," "O Come, O Come, Emmanuel," "Hail to the Lord's Anointed," "The People That in Darkness Sat," *and* "There's a Voice in the Wilderness Crying" *(BOH) are especially appropriate. If the hymn is to be an entrance song with procession, it precedes the greeting. See Appendix 2 for other hymn suggestions.*

OPENING PRAYER

The Lord be with you.
And also with you.
Let us pray: *(a brief pause)*

℣\ God of Israel,
   with expectant hearts
   we your people await Christ's coming.
As once he came in humility,
   so now may he come in glory,
   that he may make all things perfect
   in your everlasting kingdom.
For he is Lord for ever and ever. **Amen.**

or

The appropriate collect for each Sunday (see Appendix 1).

LIGHTING OF THE ADVENT WREATH

Those appointed may process to the wreath. While the candle(s) are being lighted, the appropriate texts may be read, recited, or sung. (See chapter 2 for options.) In some instances, the Advent wreath ceremony may be combined with the opening hymn, as when "O Come, O Come, Emmanuel" is used.

FIRST LESSON

First Sunday:

Isaiah 2:1-5	(Year A: 1983, 1986)
Isaiah 63:16–64:8	(Year B: 1984, 1987)
Jeremiah 33:14-16	(Year C: 1985, 1988)

Second Sunday:
    Isaiah 11:1-10   (Year A: 1983, 1986)
    Isaiah 40:1-11   (Year B: 1984, 1987)
    Malachi 3:1-4   (Year C: 1985, 1988)

Third Sunday:
    Isaiah 35:1-10   (Year A: 1983, 1986)
    Isaiah 61:1-4, 8-11   (Year B: 1984, 1987)
    Zephaniah 3:14-20   (Year C: 1985, 1988)

Fourth Sunday:
    Isaiah 7:10-16   (Year A: 1983, 1986)
    II Samuel 7:8-16   (Year B: 1984, 1987)
    Micah 5:2-5*a*   (Year C: 1985, 1988)

PSALM (HYMN or ANTHEM)
First Sunday:
    Psalm 122 or *BOH* 596   (Year A: 1983, 1986)
    Psalm 80:1-7 or *BOH* 562   (Year B: 1984, 1987)
    Psalm 25:1-10 or *BOH* 562   (Year C: 1985, 1988)

Second Sunday:
    Psalm 72:1-8 or *BOH* 577   (Year A: 1983, 1986)
    Psalm 85:8-13 or *BOH* 597   (Year B: 1984, 1987)
    Psalm 126 or *BOH* 597   (Year C: 1985, 1988)

Third Sunday:
    Psalm 146:5-10 or *BOH* 604   (Year A: 1983, 1986)
    Luke 1:46*b*-55 or *BOH* 612   (Year B: 1984, 1987)
    Isaiah 12:2-6 or *BOH* 612   (Year C: 1985, 1988)

Fourth Sunday:
    Psalm 24 or *BOH* 561   (Year A: 1983, 1986)
    Psalm 89:1-4, 19-24 or *BOH* 561   (Year B: 1984,
                                                   1987)
    Psalm 80:1-7 or *BOH* 561   (Year C: 1985, 1988)

SECOND LESSON
First Sunday:
    Romans 23:11-14   (Year A: 1983, 1986)

I Corinthians 1:3-9	(Year B: 1984, 1987)
I Thessalonians 3:9-13	(Year C: 1985, 1988)

Second Sunday:

Romans 15:4-13	(Year A: 1983, 1986)
II Peter 3:8-15a	(Year B: 1984, 1987)
Philippians 1:3-11	(Year C: 1985, 1988)

Third Sunday:

James 5:7-10	(Year A: 1983, 1986)
I Thessalonians 5:16-24	(Year B: 1984, 1987)
Philippians 4:4-9	(Year C: 1985, 1988)

Fourth Sunday:

Romans 1:1-7	(Year A: 1983, 1986)
Romans 16:26-27	(Year B: 1984, 1987)
Hebrews 10:5-10	(Year C: 1985, 1988)

HYMN, ANTHEM, or REFRAIN (see Appendix 2)

GOSPEL

First Sunday:

Matthew 24:36-44	(Year A: 1983, 1986)
Mark 13:32-37	(Year B: 1984, 1987)
Luke 21:25-36	(Year C: 1985, 1988)

Second Sunday:

Matthew 3:1-12	(Year A: 1983, 1986)
Mark 1:1-8	(Year B: 1984, 1987)
Luke 3:1-6	(Year C: 1985, 1988)

Third Sunday:

Matthew 11:2-11	(Year A: 1983, 1986)
John 1:6-8, 19-28	(Year B: 1984, 1987)
Luke 3:7-18	(Year C: 1985, 1988)

Fourth Sunday:

Matthew 1:18-25	(Year A: 1983, 1986)
Luke 1:26-38	(Year B: 1984, 1987)
Luke 1:39-55	(Year C: 1985, 1988)

SERMON

[CREED] *(When Holy Communion is not celebrated.)*

PRAYERS OF THE PEOPLE OR PASTORAL PRAYER
Response to each petition: **Savior of the nations, hear our prayer.**

THE PEACE
May take place in silence with restraint during the Advent season. If the Sacrament of the Lord's Supper is not celebrated, the service continues with the offering, the Prayer of Thanksgiving, the hymn, and Dismissal with Blessing.

OFFERING
The gifts may be presented during the Doxology or other song of praise and thanksgiving, with the Advent themes particularly in mind.

V

A FESTIVAL
OF LESSONS AND CAROLS:
Orders of Worship with
Introduction and Commentary

One of the most beloved English traditions of Advent
and Christmas is a form of worship known as the Festival
of Lessons and Carols. There are two principal versions—
the Advent Carol Service and the Service of Nine Lessons
and Carols, which takes place on Christmas Eve. The
pattern in both is the same: God's Word is proclaimed and
contemplated in a special sequence of readings, prayers,
and choral and congregational song. The Service of Nine
Lessons and Carols was first conceived by Archbishop
Benson for use in the Truro Cathedral at the turn of this
century. In 1918 it was simplified and adapted for use in
King's College Chapel, Cambridge, by Dean Eric Milner-
White. Advent carol services were essentially adaptations
of this basic pattern, originating in schools and colleges
where it was not possible to celebrate Christmas during
the school term.

Many different versions of these services may be found
in local churches and universities throughout the United
States and the world. The following orders are adapted
from the King's College Chapel version. Suitable variations are suggested under Alternatives. The beauty of this
form of worship is its flexibility and its musical dialogue

based upon the Christmas (or Advent) lessons. The pattern is quite simple, but elaborations may be as eloquent as available musical resources permit. Yet it may be performed with a very small choir, or even without a choir if the carols and hymns are familiar.

In many local churches the tradition of lessons and carols during late Advent or on Christmas Eve as a family-oriented service, or as an ecumenical community event involving several churches, is well-established. Congregations and choirs find that, over several years, a marvelous range of choral and congregational music may be experienced and treasured. The following suggestions serve to illustrate only some of the many possibilities and to invite further imaginative planning on the part of choirs, pastors, and worship committees.

The carols and anthems given in the first order below are suitable for Christmas Eve. If the service is planned for mid-December, however, specific attention should be paid to using Advent lessons and carols, along with appropriate choral literature. Similarly, some churches may wish to hold the service twice: first on Christmas Eve, and again on the evening of the Epiphany, as a type of concluding vespers to the whole Christmas-Epiphany cycle. In the latter case, specific Epiphany hymns and choral music should be used.

Careful planning and cooperation between musicians and pastor and/or other liturgical ministers is crucial for the integrity and depth of celebration these services may bring. A marvelous collection of choral music, carols and anthems especially suited for lessons and carols, is to be found in *Carols for Choirs*, volumes 1, 2, 3 (Oxford University Press: 1961, 1970, 1978). The texts for the original Nine Lessons and Carols are printed as an appendix to volume 1, and an order for the Advent Carol Service may be found in the appendix to volume 2. The *Oxford Book of Carols*, also published by Oxford University

Press, is another indispensible resource. Most of the music referred to in the following services can be found in one of these resources.

A SERVICE OF LESSONS AND CAROLS

ORGAN PRELUDE or
PRESERVICE INSTRUMENTAL MUSIC

PROCESSIONAL HYMN
"Once in Royal David's City" *(See text in Appendix 2).*

THE BIDDING PRAYER
Beloved in Christ, we come by this service to prepare ourselves to hear again the message of the angels, and to go in heart and mind to Bethlehem, and to see the loving-kindness of our God, and the Babe lying in a manger.

Let us therefore open the Holy Scriptures and read the earliest tale of that disobedience to God's holy will, which is common to us all; and then the story of the birth of Jesus Christ our Lord, to save us from our sins and make us pure and happy; and let us thank him with our carols of praise.

But first let us pray for the needs of this whole world; and especially for peace and goodwill among all people; that they may learn to love one another, as children of one God and Father of all.

And because this would most rejoice his heart, let us remember before him the poor and helpless; the cold, the hungry and the oppressed; the sick and they that mourn; the lonely and the unloved; the aged and the little children; and all who know not the Lord Jesus, or who love him not, or who by sins have grieved his heart.

Lastly let us remember before God all those who rejoice with us, but upon another shore and in a greater

light, that multitude which no one can number, with
whom, in this Lord Jesus, we evermore are one.

These prayers and praises let us humbly offer up to
the throne of heaven, in the words which Christ himself
has taught us.

THE LORD'S PRAYER

The Almighty God bless us with divine grace; Christ
give us the joys of everlasting life; and unto the
fellowship of the citizens above, may the King of
angels bring us all.

Amen.

HYMN

"Of the Father's Love Begotten" *(BOH)*

FIRST LESSON   Genesis 3:8-15

In the garden of Eden God announces that the seed of
woman shall bruise the serpent's head.

CAROL

"Wassail Carol"   Text: XVI century
                                                  Music: William Mathias

SECOND LESSON   Genesis 22:1-8

God promises to faithful Abraham that the nations of the
earth shall call his seed blessed.

HYMN

"O Come, O Come, Emmanuel" *(BOH)*
                                                  Veni Emmanuel

THIRD LESSON   Isaiah 9:2, 6-7

Christ's birth and kingdom are foretold by Isaiah.

CAROL

"Lo How a Rose E'er Blooming"   Michael Praetorius

FOURTH LESSON   Isaiah 11:1-9

The peace that Christ will bring us is foreshown.

or

Micah 5:2-4
The prophet Micah foretells the glory of little Bethlehem.

CAROL
"O Little Town of Bethlehem" *(BOH)*

FIFTH LESSON   Luke 1:26-35, 38
The angel Gabriel salutes the Blessed Virgin Mary.

CAROL
"There Is No Rose"   Text: XV century English
                              Music: Benjamin Britten

SIXTH LESSON   Matthew 1:18-21
Matthew tells of the birth of Jesus.

CAROL
"The First Noel" *(BOH)*

SEVENTH LESSON   Luke 2:1, 3-7
The shepherds go to the manger.

CAROL
"Infant Holy, Infant Lowly"*(BOH)* Traditional Polish

and/or

CAROL
"Lullay, My Liking"   Text: XV century English
                             Music: Gustav Holst

EIGHTH LESSON   Matthew 2:1-11
The wise men follow the star to Jesus.

CAROL
"In the Bleak Midwinter" *(BOH)*

and/or

CAROL
"On This Day Earth Shall Ring"   Personent Hodie

NINTH LESSON   John 1:1-14
John unfolds the great mystery of the Incarnation.

CAROL
"Silent Night, Holy Night" *(BOH)*

THE COLLECT
(or suitable free prayer, or other prayers for the season)

The Lord be with you.

And with your spirit.

Let us pray:

Lord Jesus, Child of Bethlehem, who in love made
humankind, create in us love so pure and perfect that
whosoever our heart loves may be made after thy will,
in thy name, and for thy sake.

Amen.

THE CHRISTMAS BLESSING *(if appropriate)*

HYMN
"O Come, All Ye Faithful" [Adeste Fideles] *(BOH)*

DISMISSAL WITH BLESSING
(if a silent recessional is not preferred.)

May the One, who by his Incarnation gathered into one
all things earthly and heavenly, fill you with the
sweetness of inward peace and goodwill;

And the blessing of God, the love of Christ, and the
fellowship of the Holy Spirit remain with you always.

Go forth in peace and joy.

Thanks be to God, Alleluia!

CLOSING VOLUNTARY *(optional)*

ALTERNATIVE 1A

As a Christmas Eve candlelight service (when Holy Communion is not celebrated).

GATHERING
(Suitable music may be offered.)

OPENING SENTENCE
Behold, I bring you good news of great joy which will come to all people; for to you is born this day in the city of David, a Savior, who is Christ the Lord.

PROCESSIONAL HYMN
"Hail to the Lord's Anointed," *stanzas 1–3 (BOH).*

THE WORD OF PROMISE Luke 2:1-7

COLLECT
Stir up our hearts, O Lord, to make ready the way of thine only begotten Son, so that by his coming we may be enabled to serve thee with pure minds;
Through your Son Jesus Christ our Lord, who lives and reigns with you and the Holy Spirit, one God, world without end.
Amen.

(Lutheran *Service Book and Hymnal,* adapted)

CAROL(S): *Choral setting*
Hymn "The People That in Darkness Sat" *(BOH)*

[THE SERMON]

CAROL: *Choir and congregation*

THE WORD OF ANNOUNCEMENT Luke 2:8-13

COLLECT

CHORAL OFFERING

THE WORD OF ADORATION I Luke 2:15-20 and/or
Matthew 2:1-11

COLLECT *or* CONCLUDING PRAYERS

CAROL(S): *Choral settings*

RECESSIONAL HYMN
"Hark! The Herald Angels Sing" *(BOH)*

DISMISSAL WITH BLESSING

CHORAL RESPONSE and/or CLOSING VOLUNTARY

ALTERNATIVE 1B (short form)

OPENING PRAYER (*or* BIDDING PRAYER)

[CHORAL INVITATORY]

LESSONS AND CAROLS INTERSPERSED
*(The number of lessons read may vary.) John 1:1-14 is read as
the last lesson.*

[THE APOSTLE'S CREED] and/or

THE COLLECT

THE LIGHTING OF THE CANDLES
*The ministers light their candles from the Christ candle in the
Advent wreath. They then light those of the acolytes and
ushers, who in turn light those of the congregation, each
saying:*

The peace of Christ be with you.

and in response

And also with you.

HYMN
"Silent Night, Holy Night" *(BOH)*

DISMISSAL WITH BLESSING
Let us bless the Lord.

Thanks be to God!

[SILENT RECESSIONAL]

ALTERNATIVE 2

As a Sunday afternoon or evening service, late Advent through Epiphany, and featuring instrumental and/or choral music, or organ voluntary.

PROCESSIONAL HYMN
"O Come, All Ye Faithful" *(BOH)*

CAROL(S): *Choral setting*

ALTERNATIVE 3

As a Sunday morning service in Advent.

This service may be especially suitable for the third Sunday, sometimes called Rejoicing Sunday.

The pattern may be similar to the full order, or to Alternative 1. After the processional or opening hymn, it is appropriate to use the O Antiphons (see Appendix 1, or *Seasons of the Gospel*, p. 50). Responses may be in the form of a simple repeated musical phrase. The brief sermon would follow any of the readings during the last third of the service. Provision should be made for the offering of gifts, perhaps immediately following the sermon.

A final note: When congregational singing is emphasized, rather than the choral presentations of the choir, the hymns and carols can be varied in simple expressive ways. For example, in a five-stanza processional hymn, the first could be sung by the congregation, the second by the choir, the third by women (or solo voices), the fourth by men (or the choir), and the fifth by everyone. If the congregation sings well in parts, one stanza might be a cappella.

SUGGESTED LESSONS FOR ADVENT CAROL SERVICE

FIRST LESSON   Isaiah 40:1-8
The prophet proclaims good news to a people in exile.

SECOND LESSON   Jeremiah 23:5-6
  The Lord promises to send his people a righteous King.

THIRD LESSON   Zechariah 9:9-10
  The Lord promises that the King will come to Israel in
  peace.

FOURTH LESSON   Haggai 2:6-9
  The Lord promises Israel more splendor than ever
  before.

FIFTH LESSON   Isaiah 35:1-7
  The prophet foretells the advent of the Desire of all
  nations.

SIXTH LESSON   Luke 1:26-35, 38
  The angel Gabriel salutes the Blessed Virgin Mary.

SIXTH LESSON (alternative)   Romans 8:28-29
  Paul declares the good purpose of God.

SEVENTH LESSON   Mark 1:1-15
  Jesus proclaims the coming of the kingdom of God.

VI

CHRISTMAS EVE
AND CHRISTMAS DAY:
Orders of Worship with
Introduction and Commentary

Christmas Eve services have enjoyed great popularity. The candlelight service and the Christmas Eve Holy Communion have special appeal to Christians because of the environment of the night solemnity, the lights shining in the darkness, and the glorious range of music associated with the biblical themes. Christmas Eve focuses upon the profound intimacy of tender humanity and the mystery of the nativity. Many churches celebrate the Sacrament of the Lord's Supper on this evening.

In recent years increasing numbers of churches have developed, or wish to develop an early evening or late afternoon pattern of worship oriented toward families who, because of younger children, find it difficult to attend the midnight service. In the previous chapter we have given one example of a family-oriented liturgy designed as a lessons and carols service. Many variations may be developed from that simple pattern. Children's choirs or children's participation in instrumental and congregational music is particularly encouraged.

The two services for Christmas Eve which follow are flexibly designed so that the elements may be interchanged. Some churches may not hold services on Christmas Day when it does not fall on Sunday. In this event, the Scriptures, lessons, and psalms for the "First Sunday After Christmas" are in accord with those used on Christmas Eve.

CHRISTMAS EVE FAMILY SERVICE

GATHERING AND GREETING
Choral or instrumental music may be offered, especially selections based upon any of the carols and hymns to be sung by the congregation during the service. Informal singing of Christmas carols may also be appropriate.

PROCESSIONAL CAROL
Especially appropriate are "Hark! The Herald Angels Sing," "It Came upon the Midnight Clear," "Joy to the World," *and* "O Come, All Ye Faithful" *(BOH).*

OPENING PRAYER
The Lord be with you.
And also with you.
Let us pray: *(a brief silence)*
God, creator of all life,
  you made us in your image
  and sent your Son to be our flesh.
Grant us now in this glad time of his birth,
  that we, who have been born again through his grace,
  may daily find all things made new in him.
For he lives and reigns with you and the Holy Spirit.
Amen.

[LIGHTING OF THE ADVENT AND CHRISTMAS CANDLES]
This may take place at the conclusion of informal carol singing, if there is to be no procession. While those who will light the

candles move toward the wreath, or as each candle is lighted, the congregation and choir(s) sing:

1. Light one candle for hope,
   One bright candle for hope.
   He brings hope to ev'ry heart,
   He comes, he comes!

2. Light one candle for peace,
   One bright candle for peace,
   He brings peace to ev'ry heart,
   He comes, he comes!

3. Light one candle for joy.
   One bright candle for joy.
   Ev'ry nation will find salvation,
   In Bethl'em's baby boy.

4. Light one candle for love,
   One bright candle for love.
   He brings love to ev'ry heart,
   He comes, he comes!
   (repeat last two lines)

RESPONSE TO LIGHTING OF THE CHRIST CANDLE
Jesus Christ is the Light of the world!
A light no darkness can extinguish.

or

A hymn may be sung: "Break Forth, O Beauteous Heavenly Light" *or* "Light of the World," *stanza 1 or 3 (BOH), or refrain from* "Go, Tell It on the Mountain" *(SZ)*

PRAYER FOR ILLUMINATION
Lord, open our minds and hearts
by the power of your Holy Spirit,

that we may hear and rejoice
in the Gospel of our Savior's birth,
told in story and song this night.
Amen.

ALTERNATIVE 1

STORY or READING

ANTHEM or CAROL
(focusing on response to the story of the Scripture lesson)

STORY or READING

ANTHEM

STORY or READING

CAROL

[GOSPEL and SERMON]
(if not already incorporated into the pattern)

OFFERING
Appropriate music by choir(s) may be offered, or a psalm by song leader, with congregation responding with Antiphon—especially Psalm 96, 97, or 98. See Appendix 3.

CHRISTMAS PRAYERS
Petitions may be given, with the congregation responding:
In the name of Lord Jesus, hear us.

CONCLUDING COLLECT
O God, you have caused this holy night to shine
with the brightness of the true Light:
Grant that we, who have known
the mystery of that Light on earth,
may also enjoy him perfectly in heaven,
where with you and the Holy Spirit
he lives and reigns,
one God, in glory everlasting.
Amen.

and / or

LORD'S PRAYER

CAROL
"Joy to the World" *(BOH)*

DISMISSAL WITH BLESSING
Go in peace, go in joy
to serve God and neighbor in all that you do.
We are sent in the name of the Christ Child.
The peace of God which passes all understanding,
keep your hearts and minds in the knowledge and
love of God,
and of his Son Jesus Christ our Lord;
and the blessing of God Almighty,
the Father, the Son,
and the Holy Spirit,
be among you and remain with you always.
Amen. Thanks be to God!

ALTERNATIVE 2

FIRST LESSON
Isaiah 9:2-7   (All Years)

PSALM or ANTHEM
Psalm 96 or BOH 583   (All Years)

SECOND LESSON
Titus 2:11-14   (All Years)

ALLELUIA (ANTHEM, HYMN or CANTICLE)

GOSPEL
Luke 2:1-20   (All Years)

SERMON
A short Cantata may be offered as the proclamation

CHRISTMAS PRAYERS AND OFFERING

[LIGHTING OF THE ADVENT AND
CHRISTMAS CANDLES]

HYMN
"Joy to the World" (BOH)
(May be used as offertory song if the Holy Communion is
celebrated, in which case the gifts of bread and wine are
presented with the other gifts.)

GREAT THANKSGIVING
The Lord be with you.
And also with you.
Lift up your hearts.
We lift them to the Lord.
Let us give thanks to the Lord our God.
It is right to give him thanks and praise.
Father, at this blessed Christmas feast
we give you thanks and praise.

You created light out of darkness
and brought forth life on the earth.
You made us in your image;
and though we all have sinned
and fallen short of your glory,
you loved the world so much
you gave your only Son Jesus Christ
to be our Savior.

As Mary and Joseph went from Galilee to Bethlehem
and there found no room,
so Jesus went from Galilee to Jerusalem
and was despised and rejected.
As in the poverty of a stable Jesus was born,
so from suffering and death
you raised him to bring us life.

Therefore,
with the angels who sang
glory to you in the highest

and peace to your people on earth,
with your people in all ages
and the whole company of heaven,
we join in the song of unending praise,
singing (saying):

Holy, holy, holy Lord,
God of power and might,
heaven and earth are full of your glory.
Hosanna in the highest.
Blessed is he who comes in the name of the Lord.
Hosanna in the highest.

Truly holy are you,
and blessed is your Son Jesus Christ.
As your Word became flesh,
born of woman on that night long ago,
so on the night he offered himself up for us
he took bread,
gave thanks to you,
broke the bread,
gave it to his disciples, and said:
"Take, eat;
this is my body which is given for you.
Do this in remembrance of me."

When the supper was over
he took the cup,
gave thanks to you,
gave it to his disciples, and said:
"Drink from this, all of you;
for this is my blood of the new covenant,
poured out for you and for many,
for the forgiveness of sins.
Do this, as often as you drink it,
in remembrance of me."

Therefore,
in remembrance of all your mighty acts in Jesus Christ,

we ask you to accept this
our sacrifice of praise and thanksgiving,
which we offer in union with Christ's sacrifice for us,
as a living and holy surrender of ourselves.

Send the power of your Holy Spirit on us
and on these gifts,
that in the breaking of this bread
and the drinking of this wine
we may know the presence of the living Christ;
be one body in him, cleansed by his blood;
faithfully serve him in the world;
and look forward to his coming
in final victory.

Through him, with him, in him,
in the unity of the Holy Spirit,
all honor and glory is yours,
Almighty God,
now and for ever.
Amen.

BREAKING THE BREAD

COMMUNION
(Appropriate carols may be sung during Communion.)

PRAYER AFTER COMMUNION
We give you thanks, most gracious God,
for allowing us to share in this feast as your family
and to be fed with the bread of heaven;
Give us grace that we all may grow in love,
glorifying you in all things;
Through Jesus Christ our Lord.
Amen.

HYMN or CAROL
"Joy to the World" *or* "Angels We Have Heard on High"
(BOH)

DISMISSAL WITH BLESSING
Go in peace and joy to love and serve the Lord.
We are sent in the name of the Christ Child.
Let us bless the Lord.
Thanks be to God! Alleluia!

CHRISTMAS EVE: HOLY COMMUNION

GATHERING
When no procession is held, a simple greeting may be given
following appropriate music:
Jesus Christ is born!
O Come let us adore him!

HYMN AND PROCESSION
"O Come, All Ye Faithful" *(BOH)*

or

"Hark! the Herald Angels Sing" *(BOH)*

OPENING PRAYER
The Lord be with you.
And also with you.
Let us pray: *(a brief silence)*
O Christ,
your wonderful birth is meaningless
unless we are born again.
Your death is meaningless
unless we die to sin.
Your resurrection is meaningless
if only you have been raised.
Bring us now to such love for you
that we may enjoy you forever.
For all things in the heavens and on earth
are yours eternally.
Amen.

or

O God, you have caused this holy night to shine
  with the brightness of the true Light:
Grant that we, who have known
  the mystery of that Light on earth,
  may also enjoy him perfectly in heaven,
  where with you and the Holy Spirit,
  he lives and reigns,
  one God, in glory everlasting.
Amen.

ACT OF PRAISE or ANTHEM
  "Glory Be to God on High" *(BOH), or another setting for
  congregation and choir.*

[LIGHTING OF THE ADVENT AND
CHRISTMAS CANDLES]
  See previous services for alternatives.

PRAYER FOR ILLUMINATION
  Lord, open our minds and hearts
    by the power of your Holy Spirit,
    that we may hear and rejoice
    in the Gospel of our Savior,
    Jesus Christ, the Light of the world.
  Amen.

FIRST LESSON
  *The service may follow Alternative B. The lighting of the
  congregation's candles may take place immediately after the
  lighting of the Christ candle; or it may follow Holy
  Communion, the candles being extinguished after the singing
  of "Silent Night" as the concluding hymn.*

If Christmas Day does not fall on a Sunday and a service is to be held, it is appropriate to use the same pattern as for the Christmas Eve second service, omitting the lighting of the congregation's candles. Use the prayer texts which do not mention "holy night." If Christmas Day falls on Sunday, and the Christmas lessons have been used the preceding evening for a Christmas Eve service, either of the following sets of lessons may be used:

FIRST LESSON	Isaiah 62:6-7, 10-12
PSALM	97 or *BOH* 584
SECOND LESSON	Titus 3:4-7
GOSPEL	Luke 2:8-20

or

FIRST LESSON	Isaiah 52:7-10
PSALM	98 or *BOH* 585
SECOND LESSON	Hebrews 1:1-12
GOSPEL	John 1:1-14

In addition to planning for the environment and visuals mentioned in Chapter 3, the use of dance—especially in relation to processions and specific congregational actions—should be considered. A simple dance of adoration, depending upon the space, might well highlight a Christmas crêche or nativity scene *(praesepio)*. Specific symbols on the Chrismon or Jesse Tree may be used in the dance; and white, yellow, and gold in elegant textures are appropriate for the vestments and the dancers' clothing.

In planning music for these services, care should be taken to use a variety of instruments and musicians. Try not to do everything in any one service, but plan for a cumulative unfolding of many gifts. If both an early and a late evening Christmas Eve service are to be celebrated, design the music (choral, instrumental, and congregational) with the particular themes and congregations in mind. If large numbers of families with children are to be present, for example, music suitable for children is encouraged.

VII

JOHN WESLEY'S COVENANT SERVICE:

An Order of Worship with Historical Introduction and Commentary

Wesley established the covenant service as an important part of early Methodist life. His *Journal* often reveals an interest in covenanting. For example, on Christmas Day in 1747, he wrote, "Urged the wholly giving up ourselves to God and renewing in every point our covenant that the Lord should be our God." The first Methodist Covenant Service was held on August 11, 1755. Wesley wrote,

> I explained once more the nature of such an engagement and the manner of doing it acceptably to God. At six in the evening we met for that purpose at the French Church in Spitalfields. After I had recited the tenor of the covenant proposal, in the words of that blessed man, Richard Alleine, all the people stood up, in testimony of assent, to the number of about eighteen hundred persons. Such a night I scarce ever saw before. Surely the fruite of it shall remain for ever.

According to the journal, covenant services were held on a variety of occasions, but toward the end of Wesley's life they were usually celebrated on New Year's Day or on a Sunday near the beginning of the year.

Wesley drew on a number of sources for the service, but primarily on the writing of the Presbyterian minister Joseph Alleine: *Call to the Unconverted* and *Directions for Believers Covenanting with God.* Presbyterians and Baptists also carried out the tradition of establishing covenants, but Wesley claimed that the Scriptures originally established the practice. He justified his claim with passages such as Deuteronomy 26:17-18 and Jeremiah 31:31-34.

Wesley took great pains to instruct his followers in the meaning and purpose of a covenant. When he first used the service several days were spent in instructing those who would participate; later the instruction was limited to the day of the service. Only those with special tickets were allowed to participate, and the service always concluded with Communion.

In Wesley's time the service consisted of the reading of long portions of the works of Joseph Alleine, which exhorted the people to live lives completely dedicated to God. This was followed by the covenant prayer, very similar to the one used today, and the celebration of the Lord's Supper.

Although the service depends on a written form of the covenant prayer, Wesley never prepared a practical outline for the service; he merely published long sections from Joseph Alleine's writings about a covenant which included the covenant prayer. Wesley did not insert the service in the prayer book he sent to the American Methodists in 1784, nor did he supply the early Americans with instructions concerning the service. Therefore generations of American Methodists were unaware of the service, but during this century it has been introduced into United Methodist churches. *The Book of Worship for Church and Home* (1944) included a form of the service, and it was also included in the historical section of the 1964 edition, though it would not have been recognized by Wesley. The service was actually a slightly modified copy of the service being used at that time by British Methodists. Since Wesley's death the service had been greatly revised. But the covenant prayer itself had changed little through the years.

The following service borrows heavily from the British service. It is designed for use as the main service of worship on the first Sunday after the Epiphany, also called The Baptism of the Lord. You may wish to use the following introduction in John Wesley's own words, either printed on the bulletin cover or in place of the Greeting.

Dearly beloved, the Christian life to which we are called is a life in Christ, redeemed from sin by him, and through him consecrated to God. Upon this life we have entered, having been admitted into that New Covenant of which our Lord Jesus Christ is mediator, and which He sealed with His own blood, that it might stand for ever.

On one side the Covenant is God's promise that He will fulfill, in and through us, all that He declared in Christ Jesus, who is the Author and Perfector of our faith. That His promise still stands we are sure, for we have known His goodness, and proved His grace in our lives day by day.

On the other side we stand pledged to live no more unto ourselves, but to Him who loved us and gave Himself for us, and has called us to serve Him that the purpose of His coming might be fulfilled.

From time to time, we renew our vows of consecration, especially when we gather at the Lord's Table: but on this day we meet expressly, as generations of our fathers [or forebears] have met, that we may joyfully and solemnly renew the Covenant which bound them and binds us to God.

Let us then, remembering the mercies of God, and the hope of His calling, examine ourselves by the light of His Spirit, that we may see wherein we have failed or fallen short in faith and practice, and, considering all that this Covenant means, may give ourselves anew to God.

ORDER OF WORSHIP

GATHERING
Suitable music may be offered.

GREETING
Grace and peace from God our Father
and the Lord Jesus Christ.
Amen.
Come let us worship the Lord
who established a new covenant
through his son Jesus Christ.
We come in spirit and in truth.

HYMN
"O for a Thousand Tongues to Sing" *(BOH)*

PRAYER OF ADORATION
Let us pray:
Let us worship our creator, the God of love;
God continually preserves and sustains us;
we have been loved with an everlasting love;
through Jesus Christ we have been given complete
knowledge of God's glory.
**You are God; we praise you; we acknowledge you
to be the Lord.**
Let us glory in the grace of our Lord Jesus Christ.
Though he was rich, for our sakes he became poor;
he was tempted in all points as we are,
but he was without sin;
he went about doing good
and preaching the gospel of the kingdom;
he accepted death, death on the cross;

he was dead and is alive for ever;
he has opened the kingdom of heaven
to all who trust in him;
he sits in glory at the right hand of God;
he will come again to be our Judge.
You, Christ, are the King of Glory.
Let us rejoice in the fellowship of the Holy Spirit,
the Lord, the Giver of Life.
Through the Spirit we are born into the family of God,
and made members of the Body of Christ;
the witness of the Spirit confirms us;
the wisdom teaches us;
the power enables us;
the Spirit will do far more for us than we ask or think.
All praise to you, Holy Spirit.

SILENT PRAYER

LORD'S PRAYER

*FIRST LESSON
Isaiah 42:1-9 (Year A: 1984, 1987)
Genesis 1:1-5 (Year B: 1985, 1988)
Isaiah 61:1-4 (Year C: 1986, 1989)

*PSALM or ANTHEM
Psalm 29

*SECOND LESSON
Acts 10:34-43 (Year A: 1984, 1987)
Acts 19:1-7 (Year B: 1985, 1988)
Acts 8:14-17 (Year C: 1986, 1989)

*GOSPEL
Matthew 3:13-17 (Year A: 1984, 1987)
Mark 1:4-11 (Year B: 1985, 1988)
Luke 3:15-17, 21-22 (Year C: 1986, 1989)
*For New Year's Eve lessons, see commentary.

SERMON

HYMN
"Come, Let Us Use the Grace Divine" *(BOH)*

RESPONSES AND OFFERINGS

CONFESSION OF SIN
Let us humbly confess our sins to God.

O God, you have shown us the way of life
through your Son Jesus Christ.
We confess with shame our slowness to learn of him,
our failure to follow him,
and our reluctance to bear the cross.
Have mercy on us, Lord, and forgive us.
We confess the poverty of our worship,
our neglect of fellowship and of the means of grace,
our hesitating witness for Christ,
our evasion of responsibilities in our service,
our imperfect stewardship of your gifts.
Have mercy on us, Lord, and forgive us.
Let each of us in silence make confession to God.

SILENCE
Have mercy on us, Lord, and forgive us.
Have mercy on me, O God, according to
your steadfast love;
In your abundant mercy, blot out my transgressions;
thoroughly wash my iniquity from me,
and cleanse me from my sin.
Create in me a clean heart, O God,
and put a new and right spirit within me.
Now the message we have heard from God's Son
and that we announce is this: God is Light,
and there is no darkness in him.
When we live in the Light—and he is the Light—
then we have fellowship with one another,
and the blood of Jesus his Son
purifies us from every sin.

If we say we have no sin, we deceive ourselves,
   and there is no truth in us.
But if we confess our sins to God,
   he will keep his promise;
   he will forgive us all our wrongdoing.
Amen. Thanks be to God.

COLLECT

Let us pray:
Father, you have appointed our Lord Jesus Christ
   as Mediator of a new Covenant;
Give us grace to draw near with fullness of faith
   and join ourselves in a perpetual Covenant with you,
   through Jesus Christ our Lord. Amen.

THE COVENANT

In the old Covenant, God chose Israel
   to be a special people and to obey the Law.
Our Lord Jesus Christ, by his death and resurrection,
has made a New Covenant with all who trust in him.
We stand within this Covenant and we bear his name.
On the one side,
   God promises to give us new life in Christ.
On the other side, we are pledged to live,
not for ourselves, but for God.
Today, therefore, we meet to renew
   this Covenant that binds us to God.
(The people stand)
Friends, let us claim the Covenant God has made
   with his people
and accept the yoke of Christ.
When we accept the yoke of Christ,
we allow Christ to guide all that we do
   and all that we are,
and Christ himself is our only reward.
Christ has many ways for us to serve him;
some are easy, others are difficult.

Some receive applause; others bring only reproach;
some we desire to do because of our own interests;
others seem unnatural.
Sometimes we please Christ and meet our own needs;
at other times we cannot please Christ
unless we deny ourselves.
Yet Christ strengthens us and gives us the power
to do all these things.
Therefore let us make this Covenant with God our own.
Let us give ourselves completely to God,
trusting in his promises and relying on his grace.
I give myself completely to you, God.
Assign me to my place in your creation.
Let me suffer for you.
Give me the work you would have me do.
Give me many tasks,
or have me step aside while you call others.
Put me forward or humble me.
Give me riches or let me live in poverty.
I freely give all that I am and all that I have to you.
And now, holy God—Father, Son, and Holy Spirit—
you are mine and I am yours. So be it.
May this Covenant made on earth
   continue for all eternity.
Amen.

CONCERNS AND PRAYERS

THE PEACE

OFFERING

THE GREAT THANKSGIVING
The Peace of the Lord be always with you.
And also with you.
Lift up your hearts.
We lift them to the Lord.
Let us give thanks to the Lord our God.

It is right to give him thanks and praise.
Eternal God,
   you have made covenants with your people
through all generations.
You have been faithful from the beginning of time.
Therefore,
we join with all your people everywhere
as we give you thanks and praise.
Holy, holy, holy Lord,
God of power and might,
heaven and earth are full of your glory.
Hosanna in the highest.
Blessed is he who comes in the name of the Lord.
Hosanna in the highest!
We remember with thanksgiving, holy God,
that you sent your Son Jesus
to establish a new Covenant with us
through the shedding of blood on the cross.
Before his death he gathered a fellowship.
They ate at the same table with him and he taught them.
You asked your Son to give up his life
for them and for us, and he did.
He called us also to take up our cross
and to wear his yoke.
He promised to comfort this fellowship in suffering
and to be with it for eternity.
On the night his followers deserted him
he took bread,
gave thanks,
broke it,
gave it to his disciples, and said:
"Take, eat;
this is my body which is given for you."
When supper was over
he took the cup,

gave thanks,
gave it to his disciples, and said:
"Drink from this, all of you;
this is my blood that seals God's promise,
poured out for you and many,
for the forgiveness of sins."
By dying, he freed us from unending death;
by rising from the dead, he gave us everlasting life.
When we eat this bread and drink from this cup,
we experience anew
the presence of the Lord Jesus Christ,
and we look forward to his coming
in final victory.
Christ has died, Christ is risen, Christ will come again.
Holy Father,
we have freely entered into a Covenant with you
and now we again commit ourselves to live
in complete union with your Son.
Send your Holy Spirit on our fellowship
and on these gifts of bread and wine,
that as we join in this Covenant
we will truly be the Body of Christ.
By the gift of your Son, O God,
you have established a new Covenant.
Through him, with him, in him,
in the unity of the Holy Spirit,
all glory and honor is yours,
Almighty Father, now and for ever. Amen.

THE BREAKING OF THE BREAD

COMMUNION

PRAYER AFTER COMMUNION
Let us give thanks to the Lord.
Lord, we give thanks for the gift of this holy meal.
We praise you for sending your Son

that through him
we might be reconciled completely to you.
Christ sacrificed himself.
We offer the sacrifice of our lives.
Let all that we do be a response
to the sacrifice Christ made for us. Amen.

HYMN
"A Charge to Keep I Have" *(BOH)*

DISMISSAL WITH BLESSING
May the God who established a Covenant
   with those who seek to enter the kingdom
   be always present with you.
Amen.
May Jesus Christ, who sealed the new Covenant
   with his sacrifice on the cross, bring you peace.
Amen.
May God's Holy Spirit guide your life.
Amen.
Go in peace to serve God and your neighbor
   in all that you do.
Amen. Thanks be to God.

The Covenant Service is recommended for use as the main service on the first Sunday after the Epiphany. This Sunday is also the celebration of The Baptism of the Lord. However, practical considerations may suggest using it on another date. Wesley used the service as part of a Watch Night celebration when his followers gathered on New Year's Eve. The service might also be used on the first Sunday of the year, following the practice of British Methodists. During the year a Covenant Service could mark a special anniversary, such as the founding of a congregation, or it could be used on Aldersgate Sunday.

The service can easily be adapted for use on New Year's Eve. Wesley experimented with the service on this night as an alternative to more secular pastimes. Later he decided to hold the service regularly on the afternoon of the first day of the year.

When the service takes place on the first Sunday after the Epiphany, it marks a culmination of the Advent and Christmas seasons. Preparing for Christ's coming (Advent), celebrating his birth (Christmas), remembering that Christ was revealed as the Son of God (the Epiphany), and acknowledging that God called Jesus to a special purpose (The Baptism of the Lord), all prepare us for an act of corporate and individual commitment.

If the Service of Baptism, Confirmation, and Reaffirmation is to be used, it can easily be incorporated by adding it as the first act of Responses and Offerings. In this case the Renunciation of Sin and Profession of Faith can replace the Confession of Sin.

The celebration of a Covenant Service is also an appropriate time for other acts of dedication or commitment. For example, new church officers or church school staff members might be commissioned.

In most situations it will be impossible to follow Wesley's example of long periods of instruction before the service. This can be compensated for by early planning, so that Advent and Christmas celebrations naturally prepare a congregation for the Covenant Service. Announcements of the service can be worded to build greater understanding. Newsletter or Christmas mailings might interpret the service. References in Advent and Christmas sermons can show the relationship between these seasons and the renewing of the Covenant.

The lections for the First Sunday After the Epiphany are particularly appropriate for a Covenant Service. The Gospel is the story of Jesus' baptism by John. Jesus is our example. In submitting to baptism, he demonstrated his willingness to accept the work that God had called him to do. The first lection from Isaiah 42 reminds us of the work a servant is called to do and of the power of God. Peter's speech, the second lection, is a brief summary of what Christianity is all about.

If this service is to be celebrated as a Watch Night or New Year's Eve service, the following lessons are appropriate:

(Year A) Deuteronomy 8:1-10, Psalm 117, Revelation 21:1-6a, and Matthew 25:31-46;

(Year B) Ecclesiastes 3:1-13, Psalm 8, Colossians 2:1-7, and Matthew 9:14-17;

(Year C) Isaiah 49:1-10, Psalm 90:1-12, Ephesians 3:1-10, and Luke 14:16-24.

If the service is used at yet another time, Jeremiah 31:31-35, Hebrews 12:22-29, and John 15:1-8 or Matthew 11:27-30 may be used. Appropriate hymns include Charles Wesley's New Year's hymn, "Sing to the Great Jehovah's Praise," or "Where Cross the Crowded Ways of Life" and hymns for use at the Lord's Supper *(BOH)*.

At times the Lord's Supper has been omitted from this service. This was never Wesley's practice. On at least one occasion he preceded the service with Communion, but usually the service ended with Communion. The Lord's Supper should be included. The Covenant Service is actually a special form of Holy Communion, renewing our personal commitment to Christ in the baptismal covenant.

VIII

THE EPIPHANY:
An Order of Worship
with Commentary

GATHERING

Suitable instrumental or choral music may be offered as the people gather. Especially appropriate are choral preludes or variations on the major hymn or carol tunes to be sung during the service.

GREETING

The grace of the Lord Jesus Christ be with you.
And also with you.
The risen Christ is with us.
Praise the Lord!

HYMN

"As with Gladness Men of Old," "Light of the World, We Hail Thee," "Brightest and Best," "Earth Has Many a Noble City" *(BOH)*; "Where Is This Stupendous Stranger?" *(EP)*. *If this is a processional hymn, it may precede the Greeting. Especially fitting in the processional are banners with the specific images of the Magi, or other suitable Epiphany images.*

PRAYER

The Lord be with you.
And also with you.
Let us pray: *(a brief silence)*

God of all glory, by the guidance of a star you led the wise men to worship the Christ Child. By the light of faith lead us to your glory in heaven.

We ask this through Christ our Lord.

Amen.

ACT OF PRAISE

Here may be sung the "Gloria in Excelsis," *the* "Te Deum," *or any strong canticle of praise.*

FIRST LESSON

Isaiah 60:1-6 (All Years)

PSALM (HYMN or ANTHEM)

Psalm 72:1-14

O God, let the king be righteous;
Let the heir to the throne be just.

Let him plead the cause of your people, the poor,
By the letter and spirit of your own law.

Let the mountains declare,
 "God's people are innocent!"
And the hills announce, "We are setting them free!"

May he help the oppressed find justice,
Deliver the poor, and crush the exploiter.

Let him live as long as the sun and the moon,
Through all generations to come.

And let him come down like rain on the grass,
Like gentle showers sprinkling the earth.

Throughout his reign, let justice bloom
In peace and plenty, as long as the moon shall last.

Let him be king from sea to sea,
From the river Euphrates to the earth's farthest end.

Let his enemies kneel before him;
Let his foes all lick the dust.

Let kings to the north and east bring tribute;
Let kings to the south and west bring gifts.

Let all the kings bow before him;
Let all the nations serve him.

For he saves the poor when they cry for help
And saves the oppressed when no one will aid them.

He cares for the poor and oppressed
And saves the lives of the poor,

Redeeming them from oppression and violence,
Because he values their lives.

Translation by Gary Chamberlain

SECOND LESSON
Ephesians 3:1-12   (All Years)

ALLELUIA (HYMN or ANTHEM)
"I Come with Joy" *(SBH) or* "Christ, Whose Glory Fills
the Skies" *(BOH)*.

GOSPEL
Matthew 2:1-12   (All Years)

SERMON

PRAYERS FOR OTHERS
*Here may be offered a bidding prayer or pastoral prayer,
followed by petitions from the congregation, with the people
responding,* **"Lord of light, hear our prayer."**

or

Let us pray for the Church and for the world:
Grant, Almighty God, that all who confess your name
may be united in your truth, live together in your love,
and reveal your glory in the world.
(Silence)
Lord, in your mercy,
Hear our prayer.

Guide the people of this land, and of all the nations, in
the ways of justice and peace, that we may honor one
another and serve the common good.

(Silence)
Lord, in your mercy,
Hear our prayer.

Give us all a reverence for the earth as your own creation, that we may use its resources rightly in the service of others and to your honor and glory.
(Silence)
Lord, in your mercy,
Hear our prayer.

Bless all whose lives are closely linked with ours; grant that we may serve Christ in them and love one another as he loves us.
(Silence)
Lord, in your mercy,
Hear our prayer.

Comfort and heal all those who suffer in body, mind, or spirit; give them courage and hope in their troubles, and bring them the joy of your salvation.
(Silence)
Lord, in your mercy,
Hear our prayer, through Jesus Christ our Lord. Amen.

INVITATION TO THE TABLE, AND THE PEACE

Christ invites to this table all who confess faith in his promises and who intend to live as reconciled people. Let us, forgiven and accepted in Christ, exchange signs of peace and reconciliation with one another.

The peace of Christ be with you all.
And also with you.

OFFERING

Choral or instrumental music may be offered, or a simple dance sequence which ends with the presentation of the gifts of bread and wine, together with the offering. As an alternative to the Doxology, use an appropriate hymn or carol stanza such as

"Christ Is the World's Light" *(EP) or stanzas 1 and 3 of* "As with Gladness" *(BOH).*

THE GREAT THANKSGIVING
The Lord be with you.
And also with you.

Lift up your hearts.
We lift them to the Lord.
Let us give thanks to the Lord our God.
It is right to give him thanks and praise.

Blessed are you, Lord our God,
Creator and Sovereign of the universe,
our light and our salvation.
Before the mountains were brought forth
or you had formed the earth,
from everlasting to everlasting,
you alone are God.

Therefore,
with your people in all ages
and the whole company of heaven,
we join in the song of unending praise,
singing (saying):
Holy, holy, holy Lord,
God of power and might,
Heaven and earth are full of your glory.
Hosanna in the highest.
Blessed is he who comes in the name of the Lord.
Hosanna in the highest.

Truly holy are you, Father.
In the fullness of time
you revealed yourself in your blessed Son Jesus Christ,
the Light of the world.
Through him
we are saved and baptized into your service.

You sent a star to guide wise men
to the manger where the Christ was born;
and your signs and witnesses,
in every age and through all the world,
have led persons from far places to him.

In his baptism
and in his table fellowship
he took his place with sinners.
He preached good news to the poor,
proclaimed release to the captives
and recovery of sight to the blind,
set free the oppressed,
and announced that the time had come
when you would save your people.

On the night his disciples betrayed and deserted him
he took bread,
gave thanks to you,
broke the bread,
gave it to his disciples, and said:
"Take, eat;
this is my body which is given for you.
Do this in remembrance of me."

When the supper was over
he took the cup,
gave thanks to you,
gave it to his disciples, and said:
"Drink from this, all of you;
for this is my blood of the new covenant,
poured out for you and for many,
for the forgiveness of sins.
Do this, as often as you drink it,
in remembrance of me."

By the baptism
of his suffering, death, and resurrection
you gave birth to your Church.

His presence has continued with his people
as they have been baptized into him,
and in the breaking of bread
and sharing of the cup,
in Jerusalem and in all Judea and Samaria
and to the ends of the earth.

Therefore,
in remembrance of all your mighty acts in Jesus Christ,
we, who in past years have been baptized
into the death and resurrection of Christ,
now offer ourselves to you anew,
in union with Christ's sacrifice for us,
[and in renewal of our baptismal vows,]
as a living and holy surrender of ourselves.

Send the power of your Holy Spirit on us
and on these gifts,
that in the breaking of this bread
and the drinking of this wine
we may know the presence of the living Christ;
be one body in him, cleansed by his blood;
and look forward to his coming
in final victory.

Through him, with him, in him,
in the unity of the Holy Spirit,
all honor and glory is yours,
Almighty God,
now and for ever.

Amen.

THE LORD'S PRAYER

THE BREAKING OF THE BREAD
And he was known to them in the breaking of the bread.

PRESENTING THE CUP
The gifts of God for the people of God.

Here may be sung the traditional "Lamb of God" or a psalm Antiphon and verse, such as "O taste and see the goodness of the Lord" (Psalm 34:8), while the ministers and people begin the Communion sharing.

Hymns or psalms during Communion: "Christ, Whose Glory Fills the Skies," "Walk in the Light," *or* "Go, Tell It on the Mountain" *(BOH); Psalm 89:1-7 or 72, interspersed with silence.*

PRAYER AFTER COMMUNION
The Lord is with you.
And also with you.

Let us pray: *(a brief pause)*

Pour out upon us
  the spirit of your love, O Lord,
  and unite the wills of those
  whom you have fed with one heavenly food;
through Jesus Christ our Lord.
Amen.

or

You have given yourself to us, Lord.
Now we give ourselves for others.

Your love has made us a new people;
As a people of love we will serve you with joy.

Your glory has filled our hearts.
Help us to glorify you in all things. Amen.

HYMN
"Go, Tell It on the Mountain," "Heralds of Christ," or "Christ Is the World's True Light" *(BOH);* "Rise, Shine, You People" *(SBH).*

DISMISSAL WITH BLESSING
Now may our Lord Jesus Christ himself
  and God our Father,
  who loved us and gave us eternal comfort

and good hope through grace,
comfort your hearts and establish them
in every good word and deed.

Amen.

Go in peace and serve the Lord.

Amen. Thanks be to God!

POSTLUDE OR FESTIVE MUSIC

The Epiphany is to be a day of great joy for all Christians. It completes the twelve days of Christmas; more important, it is the festival of the manifestation of God's Word made flesh, honored by the gifts from all nations and peoples. This central image of the Magi bearing gifts suggests processions, banners, and a specific emphasis upon our joining the whole world in adoration and self-giving. Another image from tradition is the wedding feast at Cana: "The first of the signs by which Jesus revealed his glory" (John 2:11).

Most local churches will celebrate the Epiphany on the first Sunday in January and will use the appropriate lessons in place of those indicated for the Second Sunday After Christmas (See *Seasons of the Gospel*, pp. 57-58).

Since we strongly recommend the use of Wesley's Covenant Service on the Sunday following the Epiphany, as a time of baptismal renewal for the whole congregation, infant and adult baptisms may also take place then.

However, the Epiphany itself is an excellent day for baptism. The baptismal rite may be best celebrated following the sermon and before the Prayers of the People, or following the first or second lesson. Most churches will also celebrate Holy Communion. Since this service is likely to take more time than usual, it is helpful to announce this to the congregation ahead of time.

Planning for the music, both choral and congregational, requires a clear sense of the rhythm and focus of the service. For example, the instrumental and choral literature based upon the great Epiphany hymn, "O Morning Star, How Fair and Bright," is extensive and may be found in all ranges of difficulty. If particular psalm settings are used, such as cantor or choir with psalm tones for the people, plan to introduce such music well in advance, preferably in the early to mid-Fall. This could be done at a special evening gathering, and other new music for the Advent-Christmas cycle could be included as well. This allows time to learn the music and to explore the significance of the texts as prayer well before the actual service.

Good pastoral imagination is called for, since this service is adaptable to every situation and can be very simple or quite elaborate, depending upon the size of the church and the resources available. Remember that simple things accomplished well are more appropriate than complex and ambitious things hastily planned and carried out in anxiety. The Epiphany should express a joyous conclusion to the entire sweep of Advent-Christmas. Because Christ is the Light of the world, we have a story to tell to the nations.

IX

THE BAPTISM OF THE LORD:
An Alternative Service

The festival of the Epiphany presents us with a great richness of images concerning Jesus Christ, the Light of the world. It is truly a feast of plenty, proclaiming the manifestation of the Son of God, incarnate in human flesh. Three primary mysteries of the Christian faith are brought together: the star leading the Magi to the cradle, the baptism of Jesus in the Jordan, and the presence of Jesus at the marriage feast where water is turned to wine.

The Sundays after the Epiphany, beginning with The Baptism of the Lord and ending with The Transfiguration of the Lord, do not in themselves constitute a special season. They are "ordinary time," if you will. However, the Scripture readings continue to shine with the radiance and to sound forth echoes of the meaning of Christmas-Epiphany. Some of the music, both choral and instrumental, associated with the Epiphany may well be carried into our worship during some of the subsequent Sundays.

The first Sunday following January 6 is called The Baptism of the Lord. We have suggested that Wesley's Covenant Service be used on this occasion. However, some congregations will prefer to use the Covenant

Service as a Watch Night service on New Year's Eve or on
the evening of New Year's Day. In that case, the following
service is especially suitable for the first Sunday following
January 6.

GATHERING
*Choral or instrumental music may be offered, focusing
especially on baptismal themes and texts.*

GREETING
Ascribe to the Lord, O heavenly beings,
Ascribe to the Lord glory and strength.
Ascribe to the Lord the glory of his name.
Worship the Lord in holy array.
The voice of the Lord is upon the water.
The God of glory thunders,
   the Lord upon many waters.
The voice of the Lord is powerful.
The voice of God is full of majesty.
Let us praise the name of the Lord!

HYMN (PROCESSION)
"Blessed Jesus, at Thy Word," "Christ for the World We
Sing," "Glorious Things of Thee Are Spoken," "The
Church's One Foundation," "Christ Is Made the Sure
Foundation," "Christ Is the World's True Light" *(BOH)*;
"O Love, How Deep, How Broad, How High" *(LBW* and
SBH); "The Word Became Flesh" *(HFW)*.

OPENING PRAYER
The Lord be with you.
And also with you.
Let us pray: *(a brief silence)*
Living God,
   when the Spirit descended upon Jesus
   at his baptism in Jordan's water,
   you revealed him as your own beloved Son.

Keep us,
    your children who have been born
    of water and the Spirit,
    always faithful to him who is Lord for ever and ever.
Amen.

FIRST LESSON
    Isaiah 42:1-9   (Year A: 1984, 1987)
    Genesis 1:1-5   (Year B: 1985, 1988)
    Isaiah 61:1-4   (Year C: 1986, 1989)

PSALM (HYMN or ANTHEM)
    Psalm 29 or *BOH* 583

SECOND LESSON
    Acts 10:34-43   (Year A: 1984, 1987)
    Acts 19:1-7   (Year B: 1985, 1988)
    Acts 8:14-17   (Year C: 1986, 1989)

ALLELUIA (HYMN or ANTHEM)

GOSPEL
    Matthew 3:13-17   (Year A: 1984, 1987)
    Mark 1:4-11   (Year B: 1985, 1988)
    Luke 3:15-17, 21-22   (Year C: 1986, 1989)

SERMON

SERVICE OF BAPTISM AND/OR
BAPTISMAL REAFFIRMATION
    The presiding minister makes such of the following statements
    to the congregation as may be appropriate:

Brothers and sisters in Christ,
Through the sacrament of Baptism,
    believers and their households are initiated
    into Christ's holy Church.
We are incorporated into God's mighty acts of salvation
    and given new birth through water and the Spirit.
All this is God's gift, offered to us without cost.

Through confirmation
and through the reaffirmation of our faith,
we renew the Covenant declared at our baptism,
acknowledge God's gift to us,
and affirm our commitment to Christ's holy Church.

PRESENTATION OF CANDIDATES

A representative of the congregation presents the candidates:

I present *Name(s)* for baptism.
I present *Name(s)* for confirmation.
I present *Name(s)* for reaffirmation of faith.

The minister addresses parents or other sponsors and those candidates who can answer for themselves:

On behalf of the whole Church, I ask you:
Do you renounce the spiritual forces of wickedness,
the evil powers of this world,
and the bondage of sin?

I do.

Do you accept the freedom and power
God has given you
to resist evil, injustice, and oppression,
in whatever forms they present themselves?

I do.

Do you confess Jesus Christ as your Savior,
put your whole trust in his grace,
and promise to serve him as your Lord,
in union with the Church which Christ has won
for people of all ages, nations, and races?

I do.

The minister addresses parents or other sponsors of candidates unable to answer for themselves:

Will you nurture *these children/persons*
in Christ's holy Church
that, by teaching and example,

they are guided to respond to God's grace,
openly to profess *their* faith,
and to lead a Christian life?

I will.

*The minister addresses candidates who can answer for
themselves [and their sponsors]:*

According to the grace given to you,
> will you remain faithful *members* of Christ's holy
> Church
and serve as Christ's *representatives* in the world?
[And will you who sponsor *these candidates*
> support and encourage *them* in *their* Christian life?]

The minister addresses the congregation:

Do you as Christ's Body, the Church,
> reaffirm your own renunciation of sin
> and commitment to Christ?

We do.

Will you nurture one another
> in the Christian faith and life
> and include *these persons* now before you in your care?

**With God's help we will so order our lives
after the example of Christ
that *these persons,* surrounded by steadfast love,
may grow in the knowledge and love of God,
may be established in the faith,
and confirmed and strengthened
in the way that leads to life eternal.**

Let us join now with *these persons*
> in professing the Christian faith
> as contained in the Scriptures
> of the Old and New Testaments.

Do you believe in God the Father?
**I believe in God, the Father Almighty,
creator of heaven and earth.**

Do you believe in Jesus Christ?
I believe in Jesus Christ, his only Son our Lord.

[He was conceived by the power of the Holy Spirit
and born of the Virgin Mary.
He suffered under Pontius Pilate,
was crucified, died, and was buried.
He descended to the dead.
On the third day he rose again.
He ascended into heaven
and is seated at the right hand of the Father.
He will come again to judge the living and the dead.]

Do you believe in the Holy Spirit?
I believe in the Holy Spirit
[the holy catholic Church,
the communion of saints,
the forgiveness of sins,
the resurrection of the body,
and the life everlasting].
Amen.

THANKSGIVING OVER THE WATER
Water may be poured into the font at this time.
The Lord be with you.
And also with you.

Let us pray.
Eternal God,
when nothing existed but chaos,
your Spirit swept across the dark waters
    and brought forth light.
In the days of Noah
you saved those on the ark through water.
After the flood you set a rainbow in the clouds.
When you saw your people as slaves in Egypt,
you led them to freedom through the sea.
Their children, you brought through the Jordan
to the land which you had promised.

Sing to the Lord, all the earth.
Tell of God's mercy each day.

In the fullness of time you sent Jesus,
nurtured in the water of a womb.
He was baptized by John
and anointed by your Spirit.
He called his disciples
to share in the baptism of his death and resurrection
and to make disciples of all nations.

Declare his works to the nations,
his glory among all the people.

By the power of your Holy Spirit,
bless this gift of water
and those who receive it.
Wash away their sin
and clothe them in righteousness throughout their lives,
that, dying and being raised with Christ,
they may share in his final victory.

All praise to you, Eternal Father,
through your Son Jesus Christ,
who with you and the Holy Spirit
lives and reigns for ever.
Amen.

BAPTISM WITH LAYING ON OF HANDS
As each candidate is baptized, the minister says:
(*Name*), I baptize you in the name of the Father,
and of the Son,
and of the Holy Spirit.
Amen.

The minister places hands on the head of each person
immediately after each has been baptized and says:
The Holy Spirit work within you,
that, being born through water and the Spirit,

you may be a faithful disciple of Jesus Christ.
Amen.
When all candidates have been baptized, the congregation says:
Through baptism
   you are incorporated by the Holy Spirit
   into God's new creation
   and made to share in Christ's royal priesthood.
We are all one in Christ Jesus.
With joy and thanksgiving we welcome you
   as members of the family of Christ.

CONFIRMATION OR REAFFIRMATION OF FAITH

Water may be sprinkled toward those being confirmed or reaffirming their faith, or toward the entire congregation when there is a congregational reaffirmation of the baptismal covenant.

The minister says:
Remember your baptism and be thankful.
Amen.

The minister places hands on the head of each person being confirmed or reaffirming faith and says to each:
(Name), the Holy Spirit work within you,
   that, having been born through water and the Spirit,
   you may be a faithful disciple of Jesus Christ.
Amen.

PROFESSION OR RENEWAL OF MEMBERSHIP IN THE UNITED METHODIST CHURCH

If there are persons coming into membership in The United Methodist Church who have not yet been presented, they may be presented at this time.

The minister addresses all those coming into membership, those who have just been confirmed, or those who have reaffirmed their faith within The United Methodist Church:
As members of Christ's universal Church,
   will you be loyal to The United Methodist Church,

participating in its ministries
by your prayers, your presence,
    your gifts, and your service?
I will.

*If there are persons joining this congregation from other United
Methodist congregations who have not yet been presented, they
may be presented at this time.*

*The minister addresses all those coming into membership in the
congregation, those who have just been confirmed, or those
who have reaffirmed their faith within the congregation:*
As *members* of this congregation,
will you faithfully participate in its ministries
by your prayers, your presence,
    your gifts, and your service?
I will.

COMMENDATION AND WELCOME
The minister addresses the congregation:
Members of the household of God,
I commend *these persons* to your love and care.
Do all in your power to increase *their* faith,
confirm *their* hope,
and perfect *them* in love.

**We give thanks for all that God has already given you
    and welcome you in Christian love.
As members together with you in the Body of Christ
and in this congregation
    of The United Methodist Church,
we renew our covenant
faithfully to participate in its ministries
by our prayers, our presence, our gifts, and our service,
that God may be glorified in everything
    through Jesus Christ.**

The minister addresses those newly received:
The God of all grace,

who has called us to eternal glory in Christ,
establish and strengthen you,
that you may live in grace and peace.

One or more lay members may join with the minister in acts and words of welcome and peace.

Appropriate thanksgivings and intercessions for those who have participated in these acts should be included in the concerns and prayers that follow.

It is most fitting that this service conclude with Holy Communion, in which the union of the new members with the Body of Christ is most fully expressed. If Holy Communion is celebrated, the new members may receive first.

THE PRAYERS
If specific petitions are offered, the people may respond with **Hear us in your mercy, Lord** *to supplications and* **To you be thanks and praise** *to thanksgiving.*

THE PEACE
The peace may be initiated by the newly baptized or confirmed, or by those making special reaffirmations. Solemnity may be preserved by exchanging signs of reconciliation and love without words; or the traditional greeting may be used:

The peace of Christ be with you.
And also with you.

OFFERING
A hymn may be sung as the table is prepared: "Christian People, Raise Your Song," "How Good to Offer Thanks" *(SBH);* "We Give Thee But Thine Own" *(BOH). The first stanza only may be used if time is short.*

THE GREAT THANKSGIVING
Text is the same as that given for the Epiphany in chapter VIII.

THE LORD'S PRAYER

THE BREAKING OF THE BREAD

COMMUNION
Suitable hymns, songs, and psalms may be sung by congregation and choir, interspersed with silence.

PRAYER AFTER COMMUNION
Let us pray:
We give you thanks, most gracious God,
that you have given us your love
  in this holy Gospel feast
and have refreshed us by your Holy Spirit.
Now strengthen and defend us
  in joyful service to all the world;
Through Jesus Christ our Lord.
Amen.

HYMN
"This Is the Spirit's Entry Now," "Rejoice Ye Pure in Heart," "We Know That Christ Is Raised" *(SBH);* "We're Marching to Zion" *(SZ). There may be a procession to a place of reception for the newly baptized; if so, the hymn may follow the Dismissal with Blessing.*

DISMISSAL WITH BLESSING
Go in peace.
We are sent in Christ's name.
Now may the God of peace
  who brought from the dead our Lord Jesus,
  the great Shepherd of the sheep,
  by the blood of the eternal covenant,
  equip you with everything good,
  that you may do his will,
  working in you that which is pleasing in his sight;
Through Jesus Christ,
  to whom be glory for ever and ever.
Amen.

THE SUNDAYS AFTER
THE EPIPHANY:
Resources and Commentary

The Sundays after the Epiphany and before Lent may be as few as four or as many as eight, depending upon the variable date of Easter. Although not a special season, the Sundays beginning with The Baptism of the Lord and concluding with The Transfiguration of the Lord nevertheless give witness to the ministry and mission of Jesus Christ. Worship during these Sundays of January and February provides opportunity for proclaiming and witnessing to the concrete way God reveals Jesus, and the way Jesus as Messiah reveals God to all humanity.

These Sundays acquire their point and focus primarily from the ordering of the readings from God's Word. The Epistle lessons present Corinthians I and II in a nearly continuous sequence over the three-year cycle, thus allowing the congregation to hear and receive Paul's messages to one specific early church; January and February are natural times to assess the year just past and plan for mission and ministry. Multiple images of the life of discipleship and witness also occur in the Gospel readings to enrich such an exploration of the church's manifestation of God in Christ to the world. If this focus is given, care must be taken not to lose the sense of the whole Gospel that is the essence of the Lord's Day—each Sunday should be a "little Easter." This may be accomplished by careful choice of hymns, prayer texts, psalmody, and choral music, and the Great Thanksgiving or eucharistic prayer.

These Sundays may be given special focus also by concentrating on unfolding themes in the Gospel and Old Testament readings. Here we find an abundance of images and specific teachings which witness to the manifestation of God in the ministry of Jesus. All three years place a reading from John's Gospel on the second Sunday after Epiphany. This discloses the theological and existential meanings of Jesus for the world. Worshiping Christians who have just celebrated the renewal of their baptismal covenant in light of Jesus' solidarity with humanity in baptism now enter deeply into the story of his actions and words. What Christ did and said in the Gospels, he will do and say now—in Word and sacrament, but also in and through the salt and light of our discipleship and witness. The great prophetic images that come to us from the Jewish Scriptures during these Sundays are especially powerful in directing us to serve all humanity in righteousness, justice, and peace.

Among many Protestant traditions, this period has focused upon mission to the world. When integrated with the readings and celebrated in light of the manifestations of Christmas-Epiphany, such an emphasis in preaching and liturgy may provide an extraordinary opportunity to proclaim, pray, and celebrate the social implications of discipleship and mission—Christ's ongoing work in the world. Here there is no incompatibility between evangelical witness and involvement in the saving work of social justice, reconciliation and God's reign among the nations. Helpful resources for planning preaching and worship may be found in *Social Themes of the Christian Year: A Commentary on the Lectionary*, edited by Dieter T. Hessel (Philadelphia: Geneva Press, 1983). The Scripture readings provide a solid basis for biblical study and prayer on the work of the kingdom and our social witness to the world.

For the celebration of Holy Communion during these Sundays, you may wish to use the Great Thanksgiving on page 32, *At the Lord's Table*, for January, and others, such as those on pages 18, 20, and 22, for the Sundays in February before Lent begins. Opening prayers for each of the Sundays After Epiphany may be found in Appendix 1 of this book. A study of these collects alone will be very helpful in planning. Intercessions and the Prayers of the People should reflect the specific mission and ministries of the congregation. Forms III, IV, and VI on pages 387 through 392 of *The Book of Common Prayer* are particularly good models.

These Sundays also present an opportunity to learn hymns and songs from other ethnic and national traditions. Highly recommended for use by choirs and congregations are the following recent collections which include excellent music and texts from Asian-American, black, and Hispanic traditions: *Hymns from the Four Winds* (Abingdon Press, 1983), *Celebremos* II (U. M. Board of Discipleship, 1983), and *Songs of Zion* (Abingdon Press, 1982). Careful study of these sources by pastors, choir directors, and organists, and the selection of hymns and songs related to the themes of the Scripture lessons, sermon, and prayers, will open up a sense of the manifestation of Christ in many cultures and traditions—truly an experience of the "mission to all peoples."

As with the introduction of all music the congregation may sing, care must be taken to provide occasions for learning. A congregational hymn festival, or a more informal gathering for hymn learning, fellowship, and prayer during these weeks is encouraged. This gathering may involve two or more neighboring churches and can also be an ecumenical experience, sharing new music of faith across denominational and cultural lines.

XI

THE TRANSFIGURATION OF THE LORD:
An Order of Worship with Commentary

The Transfiguration of the Lord is celebrated on the Last Sunday After the Epiphany.

GATHERING

Suitable instrumental or choral music may be offered as the people gather.

GREETING

The Lord is Sovereign; let the people tremble.
God is enthroned upon the cherubim;
  let the earth shake.
The Lord is great in Zion; God is high above all peoples.
Proclaim the greatness of the Lord our God.
Worship God upon the holy mountain.

HYMN

"Lead On, O King Eternal," "Light of the World, We Hail Thee," "Christ Is Made the Sure Foundation," "Glorious Things of Thee Are Spoken" *(BOH);* "Christ upon the Mountain Peak," "O Wondrous Type! O Vision Fair" *(SBH).*

If the hymn is a processional, the Greeting may follow. Banners for use in the procession might suggest Christ's presence in a blaze of glory; vestments, paraments, and banners are doxological.

OPENING PRAYER

The Lord be with you.

And also with you.

Let us pray: *(a brief silence)*

O God,

who, before the passion of your only-begotten Son,
  revealed his glory upon the holy mountain:

Grant to us that we,

  beholding by faith the light of his countenance,
  may be strengthened to bear our cross
  and be changed into his likeness from glory to glory;

Through Jesus Christ our Lord,

  who lives and reigns with you and the Holy Spirit,
  one God, for ever and ever.

Amen.

or

God of glory and mercy,
  before his death in shame,
  your Son went to the mountaintop,
  and you revealed his life in glory.

When prophets witnessed to him,
  you proclaimed him your Son,
  but he returned to die among us.

Help us face evil with courage,
  knowing that all things, even death,
  are subject to your transforming power.

We ask this through Christ our Lord.

Amen.

FIRST LESSON

Exodus 24:12-18	(Year A: 1984, 1987)
II Kings 2:1-12*a*	(Year B: 1985, 1988)
Deuteronomy 34:1-12	(Year C: 1986, 1989)

PSALM (HYMN or ANTHEM)
Psalm 2:6-11 or *BOH* 584	(Year A: 1984, 1987)
Psalm 50:1-6 or *BOH* 584	(Year B: 1985, 1988)
Psalm 99:1-5 or *BOH* 584	(Year C: 1986, 1989)

Antiphon: **Sing the glory of the Lord forever!**

SECOND LESSON
II Peter 1:16-21	(Year A: 1984, 1987)
II Corinthians 3:12–4:2	(Year B: 1985, 1988)
II Corinthians 4:3-6	(Year C: 1986, 1989)

HYMN, ANTHEM, or CANTICLE
"We Praise Thee, O God," *BOH*

GOSPEL
Matthew 17:1-9	(Year A: 1984, 1987)
Mark 9:2-9	(Year B: 1985, 1988)
Luke 9:28-36	(Year C: 1986, 1989)

SERMON

PRAYERS

The minister may offer prayer and invite the petitions of the congregation, after each of which all respond: **Christ in glory, hear our prayer** *or* **Look upon us in mercy, Lord.**

or

Minister and people responsively

Father, we pray for your holy Church;
That we all may be one.

Grant that every member of the Church may truly and humbly serve you;
That your name may be glorified by all people.

We pray for all who govern and hold authority in the nations of the world;
That there may be justice and peace on the earth.

Give us grace to do your will in all we undertake;
That our works may find favor in your sight.

Have compassion on those who suffer from any grief or
    trouble;
That they may be delivered from their distress.

Give to the departed eternal rest;
Let light perpetual shine upon them.

We praise you for your saints who have entered into joy;
May we also come to share in your heavenly kingdom.

Let us pray for our own needs and those of others.
(silence)

THE LORD'S PRAYER
*If Holy Communion is celebrated, this may follow the Great
Thanksgiving.*

THE PEACE
*If Holy Communion is celebrated, the following invitation may
be given before the peace is exchanged:*
Christ invites to his table all who confess their faith in
    him and intend to lead a life of love and faithful
    service, seeking reconciliation, justice, and peace
    among all peoples.
The peace of Christ be with you all.
And also with you.
All exchange signs of peace and reconciliation.

OFFERING
*Choral or instrumental music may be offered, or a dance
sequence which ends with the presentation of the gifts of bread
and wine with the offering. The image of Christ in glory with
the prophets may be used.*

*If Holy Communion is not celebrated, the service may conclude
with a prayer of thanksgiving, a hymn, and Dismissal with
Blessing.*

THE GREAT THANKSGIVING

The Lord be with you.
And also with you.
Lift up your hearts.
We lift them to the Lord.
Let us give thanks to the Lord our God.
It is right to give him thanks and praise.

It is truly right to glorify you, Father,
and to give you thanks;
for you alone are God, living and true,
dwelling in light inaccessible
from before time and for ever.

Fountain of life and source of all goodness,
you made all things and fill them with your blessing;
you created them to rejoice
in the splendor of your radiance.

Countless throngs of angels stand before you
to serve you night and day;
and, beholding the glory of your presence,
they offer you unceasing praise.
Joining with them, and giving voice
to every creature under heaven,
we acclaim you, and glorify your name,
as we sing (say),

Holy, holy, holy Lord,
God of power and might,
heaven and earth are full of your glory.
Hosanna in the highest.
Blessed is he who comes in the name of the Lord.
Hosanna in the highest.

We acclaim you, holy Lord, glorious in power.
Your mighty works reveal your wisdom and love.
You formed us in your own image,
giving the whole world into our care,

so that, in obedience to you, our Creator,
we might rule and serve all your creatures.
When our disobedience took us far from you,
you did not abandon us to the power of death.
In your mercy you came to our help,
so that in seeking you we might find you.
Again and again you called us into covenant with you,
and through the prophets
    you taught us to hope for salvation.

Father, you loved the world so much
that in the fullness of time
you sent your only Son to be our Savior.
Incarnate by the Holy Spirit,
born of the Virgin Mary,
he lived as one of us, yet without sin.
To the poor he proclaimed the good news of salvation;
to prisoners, freedom;
to the sorrowful, joy.
To fulfill your purpose he gave himself up to death;
and, rising from the grave,
destroyed death,
and made the whole creation new.

And, that we might live no longer for ourselves,
but for him who died and rose for us,
he sent the Holy Spirit,
his own first gift for those who believe,
to complete his work in the world,
and to bring to fulfillment the sanctification of all.

When the hour had come
for him to be glorified by you, his heavenly Father,
having loved his own who were in the world,
he loved them to the end;
at supper with them he took bread,
and after giving you thanks,
he broke the bread,

gave it to his disciples, and said:
"Take, eat:
This is my Body, which is given for you."

When the supper was over,
he took the cup.
Again he returned thanks to you,
gave the cup to his disciples, and said:
"Drink from this, all of you;
this is the cup of the new covenant in my blood,
poured out for you and many,
for the forgiveness of sins."

When we eat this bread and drink this cup,
we experience anew
the presence of the Lord Jesus Christ
and look forward to his coming
in final victory.

Father,
we now celebrate this memorial of our redemption.
Recalling Christ's death
and his descent among the dead,
proclaiming his resurrection
and ascension to your right hand,
awaiting his coming in glory;
and offering to you,
from the gifts you have given us,
this bread and this cup,
we praise you and we bless you.

**We praise you, we bless you,
we give thanks to you,
and we pray to you, Lord our God.**

Lord, we pray
that in your goodness and mercy
your Holy Spirit may descend upon us,
and upon these gifts,

sanctifying them and showing them to be
holy gifts for your holy people,
the bread of life and the cup of salvation,
the Body and Blood of your Son Jesus Christ.

Grant that all who share this bread and cup
may become one body and one spirit,
a living sacrifice in Christ,
to the praise of your name.

Remember, Lord,
your one holy catholic and apostolic Church,
redeemed by the blood of your Christ.
Reveal its unity, guard its faith, and preserve it in peace.

[Remember (*Name* and) all who minister in your Church.
Remember all your people,
and those who seek your truth.
Remember (*Name* and) all
    who have died in the peace of Christ,
and those whose faith is known to you alone;
bring them into the place of eternal joy and light.]

And grant that we may find our inheritance
with [the blessed Virgin Mary,
with Patriarchs, prophets, apostles, and martyrs,
    and] all the saints who have found favor with you
    in ages past.
We praise you in union with them and give you glory
through your Son Jesus Christ our Lord.

Through Christ,
and with Christ, and in Christ,
all honor and glory are yours,
Almighty God and Father,
in the unity of the Holy Spirit,
for ever and ever.
Amen.

THE LORD'S PRAYER

THE BREAKING OF THE BREAD

COMMUNION
Hymns and psalms may be sung.

PRAYER AFTER COMMUNION
Lord,
  we give thanks for these holy mysteries
  which bring to us here on earth
  a share in the life to come,
Through Jesus Christ our Lord.
Amen.

HYMN
"Lord, Whose Love Through Humble Service," "Behold Us, Lord, a Little Space," "We Thank Thee, Lord" *(BOH);* "O Wondrous Type" *(SBH).*

DISMISSAL WITH BLESSING
Go in peace to serve God and your neighbor
  in all you do.
We are sent in Christ's name.

May the Lord make his face shine upon you
  and be gracious to you.
May the Lord look upon you with favor
  and give you peace.
Amen.

FESTIVE MUSIC

Since this is the last Sunday before Ash Wednesday, the beginning of Lent, we are presented with an opportunity to express and experience the mystery of Christ's glory that is hidden from the eyes of the world. The Sundays After the Epiphany have explored various signs of his manifestation. Today the image is of transfiguration in Christ.

The proclamation may choose to focus on the relationship between mountaintop experiences and our faithfulness in the world. Many Patriarchs and prophets of the Jewish Scriptures may be pictured in the great procession of God's messengers. Jesus is the last in the line of the biblical prophets. But there are modern prophets, as well, who may be named in our prayers and songs. For example, the last speech of Martin Luther King, Jr., with its use of *mountaintop,* reminds us that Jesus came down to the world's sin and death and faced his own obedience unto death. The service may wish to explore this tension, focusing upon God's gracious will to transform and transfigure all humanity.

If Holy Communion is celebrated, the planning team for the service should study the text of the Great Thanksgiving above for further ideas concerning music and visuals.

APPENDIXES:
Additional Resources

1. Prayers and Litanies

*COLLECTS FOR
THE ADVENT-CHRISTMAS-EPIPHANY CYCLE*

FIRST SUNDAY IN ADVENT

Almighty God, give us grace to cast away the works of darkness and put on the armor of light, now in the time of this mortal life in which your Son Jesus Christ came to visit us in great humility; that in the last day, when he shall come again in his glorious majesty to judge both the living and the dead, we may rise to the life immortal; through him who lives and reigns with you and the Holy Spirit, one God, now and for ever. **Amen.**

#2 SECOND SUNDAY IN ADVENT

Merciful God, who sent your messengers the prophets to preach repentance and prepare the way for our salvation: Give us grace to heed their warnings and forsake our sins, that we may greet with joy the coming of Jesus Christ our Redeemer; who lives and reigns with you and the Holy Spirit, one God, now and for ever. **Amen.**

THIRD SUNDAY IN ADVENT

Stir up your power, O Lord, and with great might come among us; and because we are sorely hindered by our sins, let your bountiful grace and mercy speedily help deliver us; through Jesus Christ our Lord, to whom, with you and the Holy Spirit, be honor and glory, now and for ever. **Amen.**

FOURTH SUNDAY IN ADVENT

Purify our conscience, Almighty God, by your daily visitation, that your Son Jesus Christ, at his coming, may find in us a mansion prepared for himself; who lives and reigns with you, in the unity of the Holy Spirit, one God, now and for ever. **Amen.**

CHRISTMAS EVE (DECEMBER 24)

O God, you have caused this holy night to shine with the brightness of the true Light: Grant that we, who have known the mystery of that Light on earth, may also enjoy him perfectly in heaven; where with you and the Holy Spirit he lives and reigns, one God, in glory everlasting. **Amen.**

CHRISTMAS (DECEMBER 25)

O God, you make us glad by the yearly festival of the birth of your only Son Jesus Christ: Grant that we, who joyfully receive him as our Redeemer, may with sure confidence behold him when he comes to be our Judge; who lives and reigns with you and the Holy Spirit, one God, now and for ever. **Amen.**

or

Almighty God, you have given your only-begotten Son to take our nature upon himself and to be born [this day] of a pure virgin: Grant that we, who have been born again and made your children by adoption and grace, may daily be renewed by your Holy Spirit; through our Lord Jesus Christ, to whom with you and the same Spirit be honor and glory, now and for ever. **Amen.**

FIRST SUNDAY AFTER CHRISTMAS

Almighty God, you have poured upon us the new light of your incarnate Word: Grant that this light, enkindled in our hearts, may shine forth in our lives; through Jesus Christ our Lord, who lives and reigns with you, in the unity of the Holy Spirit, one God, now and for ever. **Amen.**

SECOND SUNDAY AFTER CHRISTMAS

O God, who wonderfully created, and yet more wonderfully restored the dignity of human nature: Grant that we may share the divine life of him who humbled himself to share our humanity, your Son Jesus Christ; who lives and reigns with you in the unity of the Holy Spirit, one God, for ever and ever. **Amen.**

THE EPIPHANY (JANUARY 6)

O God, by the leading of a star you manifested your only Son to the peoples of the earth: Lead us, who know you now by faith, to your presence, where we may see your glory face to face; through Jesus Christ our Lord, who lives and reigns with you and the Holy Spirit, one God, now and for ever. **Amen.**

FIRST SUNDAY AFTER THE EPIPHANY:
THE BAPTISM OF THE LORD

Father in heaven, who at the baptism of Jesus in the River Jordan proclaimed him your beloved Son and anointed him with the Holy Spirit: Grant that all who are baptized into his name may keep the covenant they have made and boldly confess him as Lord and Savior; who with you and the Holy Spirit lives and reigns, one God, in glory everlasting. **Amen.**

SECOND SUNDAY AFTER THE EPIPHANY

Almighty God, whose Son our Savior Jesus Christ is the Light of the world: Grant that your people, illumined by your Word and sacraments, may shine with the radiance of Christ's glory, that he may be known, worshiped, and obeyed to the ends of the earth; through Jesus Christ our Lord, who with you and the Holy Spirit lives and reigns, one God, now and for ever. **Amen.**

THIRD SUNDAY AFTER THE EPIPHANY

Give us grace, O Lord, to answer readily the call of our Savior Jesus Christ and proclaim to all people the Good News of his salvation, that we and the whole world may perceive the glory of his marvelous works; who lives and reigns with you and the Holy Spirit, one God, for ever and ever. **Amen.**

FOURTH SUNDAY AFTER THE EPIPHANY

Almighty and everlasting God, you govern all things both in heaven and on earth: Mercifully hear the supplications of your people, and in our time grant us your peace; through Jesus Christ our Lord, who lives and reigns with you and the Holy Spirit, one God, for ever and ever. **Amen.**

FIFTH SUNDAY AFTER THE EPIPHANY

Set us free, O God, from the bondage of our sins, and give us the liberty of that abundant life which you have made known to us in your Son our Savior Jesus Christ; who lives and reigns with you, in the unity of the Holy Spirit, one God, now and for ever. **Amen.**

SIXTH SUNDAY AFTER THE EPIPHANY

O God, the strength of all who put their trust in you: Mercifully accept our prayers; and because in our weakness we can do nothing good without you, give us the help of your grace, that in keeping with your commandments we may please you in both will and deed; through Jesus Christ our Lord, who lives and reigns with you and the Holy Spirit, one God, for ever and ever. **Amen.**

SEVENTH SUNDAY AFTER THE EPIPHANY

O Lord, you have taught us that without love, whatever we do is worth nothing: Send your Holy Spirit and pour into our hearts your greatest gift, which is love, the true bond of peace and of all virtue, and without which whoever lives is accounted dead before you. Grant this for the sake of your only Son Jesus Christ, who lives and reigns with you and the Holy Spirit, one God, now and for ever. **Amen.**

EIGHTH SUNDAY AFTER THE EPIPHANY

Most loving Father, whose will it is for us to give thanks for all things, to fear nothing but the loss of you, and to cast all our care on you who care for us: Preserve us from faithless fears and worldly anxieties, that no clouds of this mortal life may hide from us the light of that love which is immortal, and which you have manifested to us in your Son Jesus Christ our Lord; who lives and reigns with you, in the unity of the Holy Spirit, one God, now and for ever. **Amen.**

LAST SUNDAY AFTER THE EPIPHANY: THE TRANSFIGURATION OF THE LORD

O God, who before the passion of your only-begotten Son revealed his glory upon the holy mountain: Grant to us that we, beholding by faith the light of his countenance, may be strengthened to bear our cross and be changed into his likeness from glory to glory; through Jesus Christ our Lord, who lives and reigns with you and the Holy Spirit, one God, for ever and ever. **Amen.**

A LITANY OF THANKSGIVING

Let us give thanks to God our Creator for all the gifts so freely bestowed upon us: *(a brief silence)*
For the beauty and wonder of creation, in earth and sky and sea,
We thank you, Lord.

For all that is gracious in the lives of men and women, revealing the image of Christ,
We thank you Lord.

For our daily food and drink, our homes and families, and our friends,
We thank you, Lord.

For minds to think, and hearts to love, and hands to serve,
We thank you, Lord.

For health and strength to work, and leisure to rest and play,
We thank you, Lord.

For the brave and courageous, who are patient in suffering and faithful in adversity,
We thank you, Lord.

For all valiant seekers after truth, liberty, justice, and peace,
We thank you, Lord.

For the communion of saints, in all times and places,
We thank you, Lord.

Above all, let us give thanks for the great promises and mercies given to us and to all the world in Christ Jesus our Lord;
To Christ be praise and glory, with the Father and the Holy Spirit, now and for ever. Amen.

THE O ANTIPHONS

For at least nine centuries, and perhaps much longer, the Church has sung a solemn antiphon on each of the last seven days of preparation for Christmas. At the hour of vespers, wherever the liturgy of praise is sung in the West, the grave, pleading, confident song of these ancient antiphons rises to the Desired of the Nations.

Embodying the very heart of all the Advent liturgy, each of these prayers addresses the Lord by one of the great scriptural titles: O Wisdom, Adonai, Root of Jesse, Emmanuel. . . . Each ends with a plea for Christ's coming now in grace and, in the fullness of time, in glory: Come, and teach us. Come, and save us. Come, and deliver us. . . .

This translation, older and slightly more elaborate, is an alternate version of the Advent Antiphons presented in *Seasons of The Gospel*. These may be used in several ways: as part of the Sunday service, at the lighting of the Advent wreath candles; as part of the intercessions; or as part of special Sunday or week-night vespers during the last week of Advent. They may be read in unison, or the final refrain may be a congregational response: "Come . . ."

O ADONAI

O Adonai and Leader of the house of Israel, who appeared to Moses in the flames of the burning bush and gave him the Law on Sinai: come, and with your outstretched arm redeem us.

O WISDOM

O Wisdom, who came forth from the mouth of the Most High, reaching from end to end and ordering all things mightily and sweetly: come, and teach us the way of prudence.

O ROOT OF JESSE

O Root of Jesse, who stands for an ensign of the people, before whom kings shall keep silence and to whom the Gentiles shall make their supplication: come, deliver us and tarry not.

O KEY OF DAVID

O Key of David and Scepter of the House of Israel, who opens and no one shuts, who shuts and no one opens: come, and bring forth from prison the captive who sits in darkness and in the shadow of death.

O DAYSPRING

O Dayspring, Brightness of the Light eternal and Sun of Justice: come, and enlighten those who sit in darkness and in the shadow of death.

O KING OF THE GENTILES

O King of the Gentiles and their Desired One, Cornerstone that makes both one: come, and deliver us whom you formed out of the dust of the earth.

O EMMANUEL

O Emmanuel, our King and Lawgiver, the Expected of the nations and their Savior: come to save us, O Lord, our God.

VERSICLES

(Suitable for concluding intercessions or other prayers. A simple musical setting may be found in Praise God in Song: Ecumenical Daily Prayer *[Chicago: G.I.A. Publications, 1979], p. 37.)*

In you, O Lord, is the source of life.
In your light we shall see light.
Send forth your light and your truth.
Let these be our guide.
Fill us each morning with your constant love.
That we may sing and be glad all our life.
Let us see your mighty acts.
May your children see your glorious might.

Lord our God, may your blessing be upon us.
And give us success in all we do.

2. Supplemental Hymn Texts

See the *Resource Collection of Hymns and Service Music for the Liturgy,* prepared by the International Commission on English in the Liturgy (G.I.A. Publications, 7404 South Mason Avenue, Chicago, IL 60638).

This collection contains an excellent set of hymns in the common domain which may be reproduced in service bulletins directly from the book. Hymns for Advent, Christmas-Epiphany, and The Baptism of the Lord are numbers 1–36. Note also hymns for All Saints' Day, (205), and especially hymns and service music (251–271), along with common responses and psalm settings for Advent and Christmas (275–278 and 296).

FOR ADVENT

"THE ADVENT OF OUR GOD" *(LBW)*

1. The advent of our God
   Shall be our theme for prayer;
   Come let us meet him on the road
   And place for him prepare.

2. The everlasting Son
   Incarnate stoops to be,
   Himself the servant's form puts on
   To set his people free.

3. Come, Zion's daughter, rise
   To meet your lowly king,
   Nor let your faithless heart despise
   The peace he comes to bring.

4. As judge, on clouds of light,
   He soon will come again,
   And all his scattered saints unite
   With him on high to reign.

5. Before the dawning day
   Let sin be put to flight;
   No longer let the law hold sway,
   But walk in freedom's light.

6. All glory to the Son,
   Who comes to set us free,
   With Father, Spirit, ever one
   Through all eternity.

FOR FEAST OF CHRIST THE KING OR
THE TRANSFIGURATION OF THE LORD

"O GOD OF GOD, O LIGHT OF LIGHT" (LBW)
(O GROSSER GOTT [LMD])

1. O God of God, O Light of light,
   O Prince of Peace and King of kings:
   To you in heaven's glory bright
   The song of praise forever rings.
   To him who shares the Father's throne,
   The Lamb once slain but raised again,
   Be all the glory he has won,
   All thanks and praise! Amen. Amen.

2. For deep in prophets' sacred page,
   And grand in poets' winged word,
   Slowly in type, from age to age
   The nations saw their coming Lord;
   Till through the deep Judean night
   Rang out the song, "Good will to men!"
   Sung once by first-born sons of light,
   It echoes now, "Goodwill!" Amen.

3. That life of truth, those deeds of love,
   That death so steeped in hate and scorn—
   These all are past, and now above
   He reigns, our king first crowned with thorn.
   Lift up your heads, O mighty gates!
   So sang that host beyond our ken.
   Lift up your heads, your king awaits.
   We lift them up. Amen. Amen.

4. Then raise to Christ a mighty song
   And shout his name, his glories tell!
   Sing, heav'nly host, your praise prolong,
   And all on earth, your anthem swell!
   All hail, O Lamb for sinners slain!
   Forever let the song ascend!
   All hail, O Lamb enthroned to reign!
   All hail! All hail! Amen! Amen!

FOR FESTIVAL OF LESSONS AND CAROLS

"ONCE IN ROYAL DAVID'S CITY"

1. Once in royal David's city
   Stood a lowly cattle shed,
   Where a mother laid her baby
   In a manger for his bed:
   Mary was that mother mild,
   Jesus Christ her little child.

2. He came down to earth from heaven,
   Who is God and Lord of all,
   And his shelter was a stable,
   And his cradle was a stall;
   With the poor, and mean, and lowly,
   Lived on earth our Saviour holy.

3. And, thro' all his wondrous childhood,
   He would honor and obey,
   Love, and watch the lowly maiden
   In whose gentle arms he lay;
   Christian children all must be
   Mild, obedient, good as he.

4. For he is our childhood's pattern;
   Day by day like us he grew;
   He was little, weak, and helpless,
   Tears and smiles like us he knew;
   And he feeleth for our sadness,
   And he shareth in our gladness.

5. And our eyes at last shall see him,
   Through his own redeeming love;
   For that child so dear and gentle
   Is our Lord in heav'n above;
   And he leads his children on
   To the place where he is gone.

6. Not in that poor lowly stable,
   With the oxen standing by,
   We shall see him; but in heaven,
   Set at God's right hand on high;
   When like stars his children crowned,
   All in white shall wait around.

Other hymnbooks and collections to be consulted:
   Songs of Zion (Abingdon Press)
   Hymns from the Four Winds (Abingdon Press)
   Supplement to The Book of Hymns (Abingdon Press)
   Ecumenical Praise (Agape, Hope Publishing)
   Lutheran Book of Worship (Augsburg)
   Carols for Choirs, 1, 2, 3 (Oxford)
   Oxford Book of Carols (Oxford)

3. Psalmody

The following collections present a wide variety of the best resources for psalm settings for worship now available. All are composed for congregation with cantor and choir. *Music From Taizé*, by J. Berthier, also contains a marvelous range of responses, litanies, and acclamations suitable for the entire church year.

Alive Now! July/August 1981; July/August 1983. These issues are special editions devoted to new psalm settings.

Benedictine Book of Song. Koopmann, Robert, O.S.B., et al., eds. Collegeville, Minn.: The Liturgical Press, 1980.

Biblical Hymns and Psalms. Vols. 1, 2. Deiss, Lucien, C.S.Sp. Cincinnati: World Library Publications, 1973.

Cantor-Congregation Series. Chicago: G.I.A. Publications, 1982 and continuing.

ICEL Lectionary Music: Psalms and Alleluia and Gospel Acclamations for the Liturgy of the Word. Chicago: G.I.A. Publications, 1982.

Music from Taizé. Berthier, Jacques. Chicago: G.I.A. Publications, 1980. Vocal and instrumental editions.

Praise God in Song. Storey, William, and Melloh, John, S.M. Chicago: G.I.A. Publications, 1979.

Psalms for the Church Year: For Congregation and Choir. Minneapolis: Augsburg Publishing House, 1975.

Psalms for Feasts and Seasons: Settings of the Common Responsorial Psalms. Willcock, Christopher, S.J. Glendale, Ariz.: Pastoral Arts Associates of North America, 1979.

Psalms of the Elements: 20 Responsorial Psalms. Williamson, Malcolm. New York: Boosey & Hawkes, 1976.

Swayed Pines Song Book. Hays, Henry Bryan, O.S.B. Collegeville, Minn.: Liturgical Press, 1981.

Twenty-four Psalms and a Canticle; Thirty Psalms and Two Canticles; etc. Gelineau, Joseph, S.J. Chicago: G.I.A. Publications, 1967.